Born in the year
Geboren im Jahr

1974

Astrological character profiles
for every day of the year

Astrologische Charakterprofile
für jeden Tag des Jahres

Bibliografische Information der Deutschen Nationalbibliothek:
Die Deutsche Nationalbibliothek verzeichnet diese Publikation
in der Deutschen Nationalbibliografie; detaillierte bibliografische
Daten sind im Internet über http://dnb.dnb.de abrufbar.

christoph.daeppen@bluewin.ch

Herstellung und Verlag:
BoD – Books on Demand, Norderstedt

ISBN 9783746059334

The present paper contains diagrams of the astrological determined character profiles for every day of the year 1974. The data points in the diagrams are depicting the manifestations regarding the following character traits in the scheme of the so-called „Big Five" of psychology:

N: Neuroticism
E: Extraversion
O: Openness (to Experience)
A: Agreeableness
C: Conscientiousness

The underlying astrological model and the applied methods of calculation used for these diagrams are described in a separate work. $(\rightarrow \S)$

The diagrams have two scales: one is „absolute" (left) and one is „relative" (right). The data points connected with the solid line relate to the absolute scale; those connected with the dotted line relate to the relative, i.e. percent scale. The relative value thus shows the percentage of the corresponding absolute value compared to the sum of all absolute values deviating from the average or zero line. Values above the average line express higher manifestations of the corresponding character trait and vice versa. The lines connecting the dots have no special meaning except for the purpose of helping to visualize the data points and their spatial distribution within the diagram. The calculation method for determing the absolute values (based on the Swiss Ephemeris tables) is described in the work mentioned above.

The diagrams exhibited as follows do not imply any propositions beyond the findings and considerations that have been made in the work mentioned above, especially regarding the possibility of gender related differences. Readers are invited to critically examine and openly discuss the revealed diagrams in terms of significance, accuracy and further possible use.

Das vorliegende Werk enthält die Diagramme der astrologischen Charakterprofile für jeden Tag des Jahres 1974. Die Datenpunkte in den Diagrammen zeigen die Ausprägungen hinsichtlich folgender Charaktereigenschaften im Schema der sogenannten „Big Five" der Psychologie:

N:	Neuroticism	- Neurotizismus
E:	Extraversion	- Extraversion
O:	Openness (to Experience)	- Offenheit (für Erfahrungen)
A:	Agreeableness	- Verträglichkeit
C:	Conscientiousness	- Rigidität

Das den Diagrammen zugrunde liegende astrologische Modell und die applizierten Berechnungsmethoden sind in einer separaten Studie beschrieben. (→ § ; siehe dort auch die deutschen Fachbegriffe)

Die Diagramme haben zwei Skalen: eine „absolute" (links) und eine „relative" (rechts). Die mit der ausgezogenen Linie verbundenen Datenpunkte beziehen sich auf die absolute Skala; jene mit der gestrichelten Linie verbundenen beziehen sich auf die relative, d.h. prozentuale Skala. Der relative Wert drückt somit aus, welcher prozentuale Anteil der entsprechende absolute Wert an der Summe aller absoluten Wertabweichungen von der Null- bzw. Mittellinie hat. Werte über der Mittellinie indizieren höhere Ausprägungen des betreffenden Charaktermerkmals und Werte darunter entsprechend tiefere. Die die Punkte verbindenden Linien haben selber keine spezielle Bedeutung, sie dienen lediglich der Visualisierung der Datenpunkte bezüglich ihrer räumlichen Verteilung im Diagramm. Die Methode zur Berechnung der absoluten Werte (basierend auf den Swiss Ephemeris Tabellen) ist in der erwähnten Studie beschrieben.

Die im folgenden vorgelegten Diagramme implizieren keine Aussagen, die über die in der oben genannten Studie präsentierten Befunde und Erwägungen hinaus gehen, insbesondere die Möglichkeit von geschlechtsbedingten Unterschieden betreffend. Die Leser sind eingeladen, die gezeigten Diagramme hinsichtlich Aussagekraft,

Treffsicherheit und weiterer Verwendungsmöglichkeit kritisch zu prüfen und offen zu diskutieren.

§ Christoph Däppen: Die Planeten der Präsidenten – Einblicke in eine neue Astrologie; BoD 2015. ISBN 978-3-7386-0655-3.

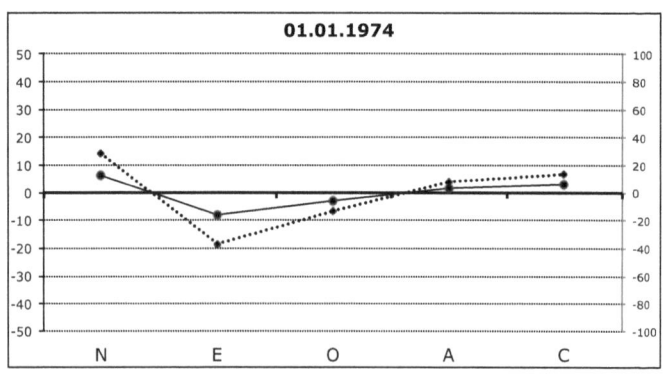

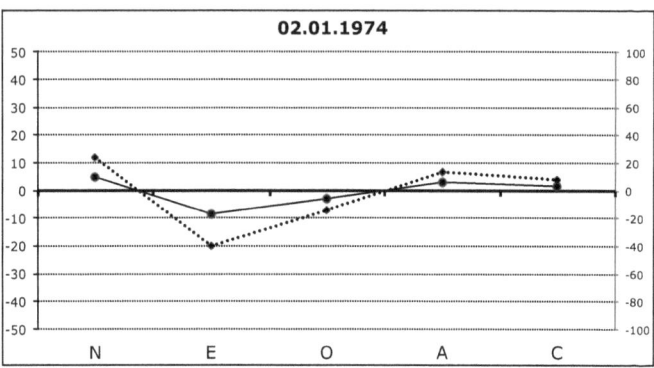

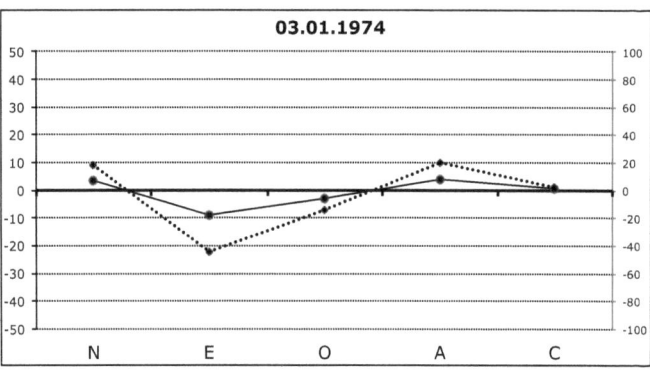

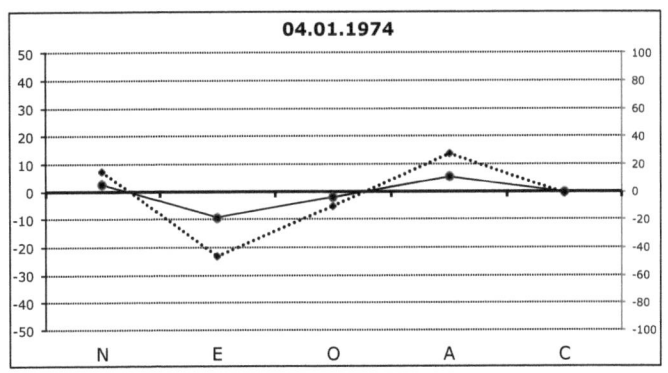

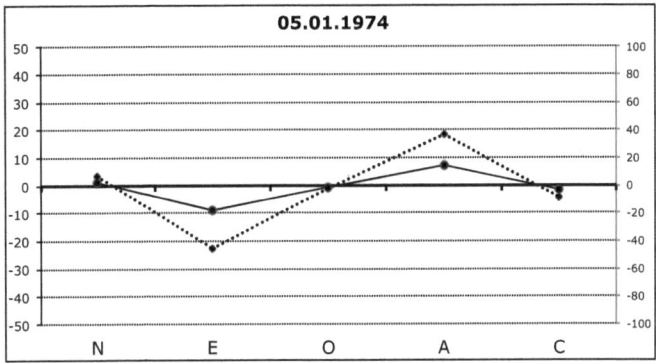

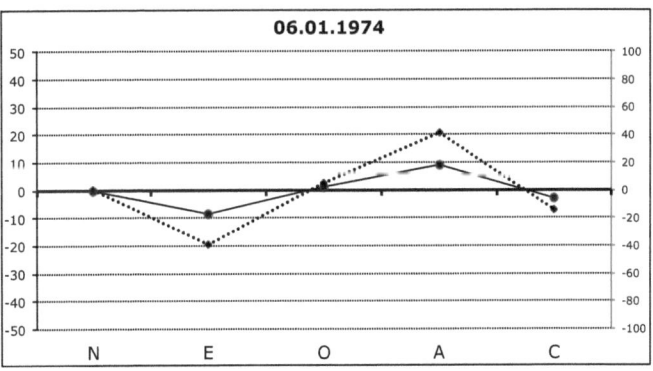

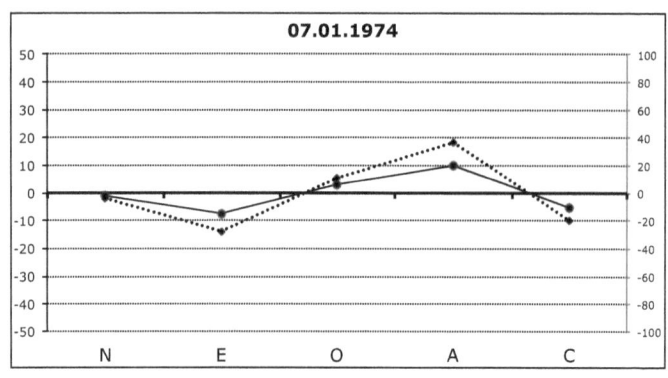

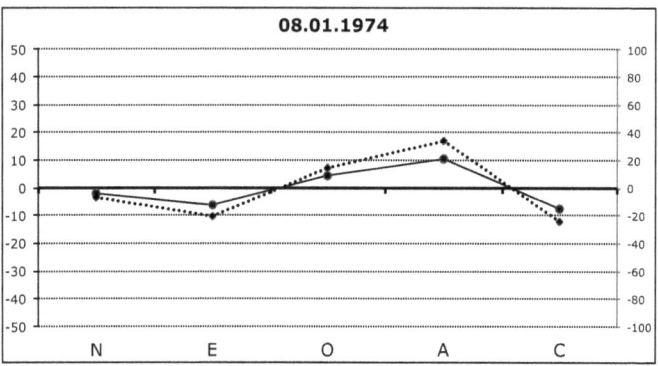

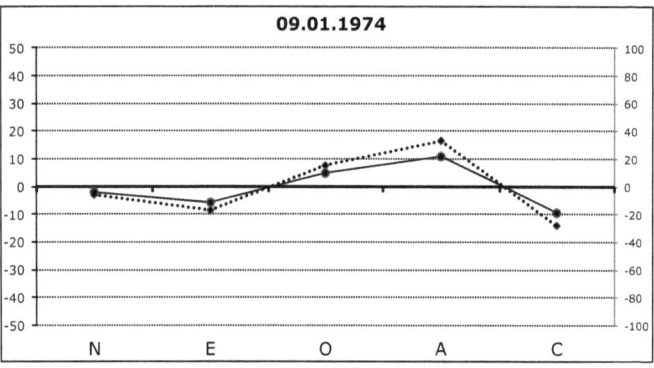

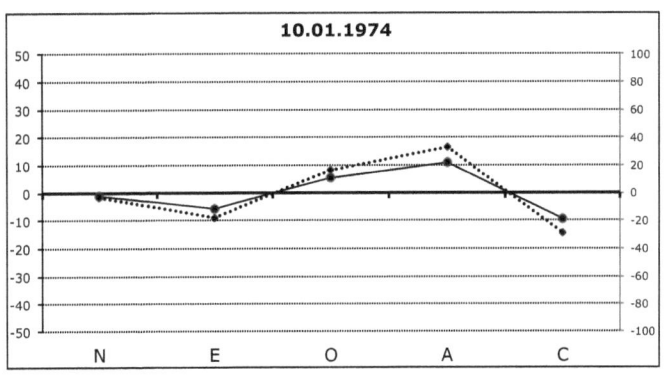

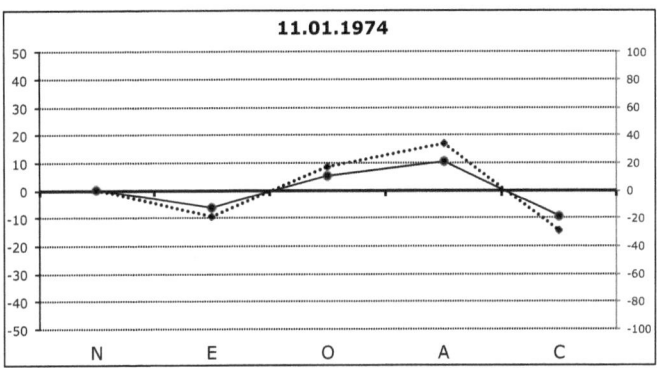

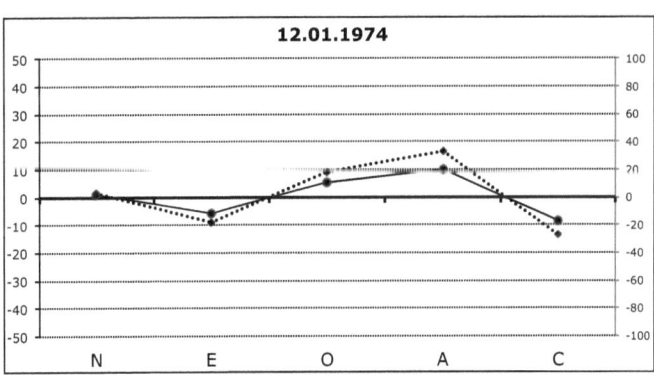

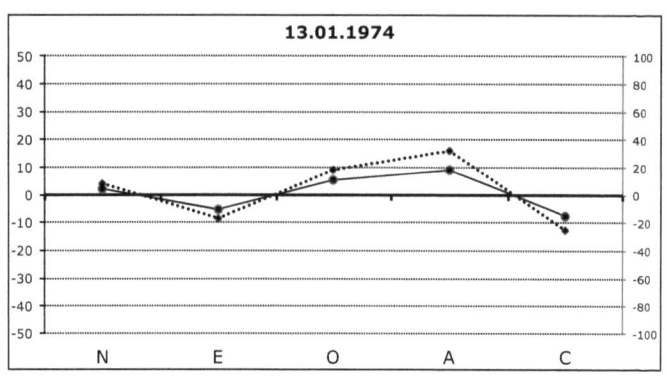

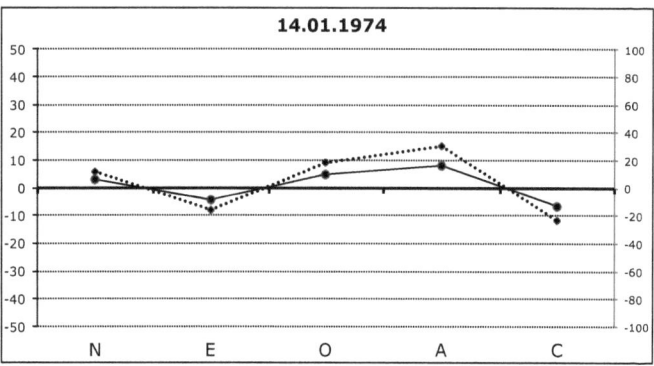

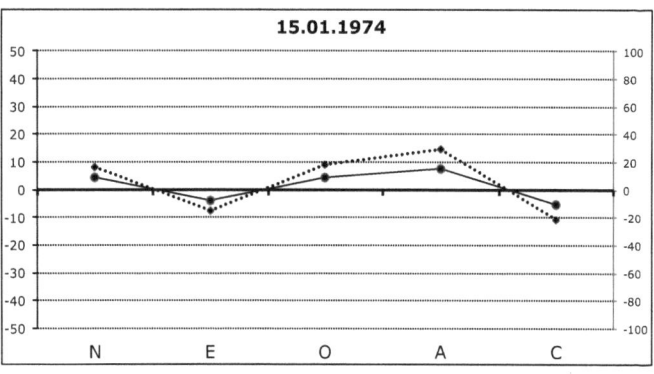

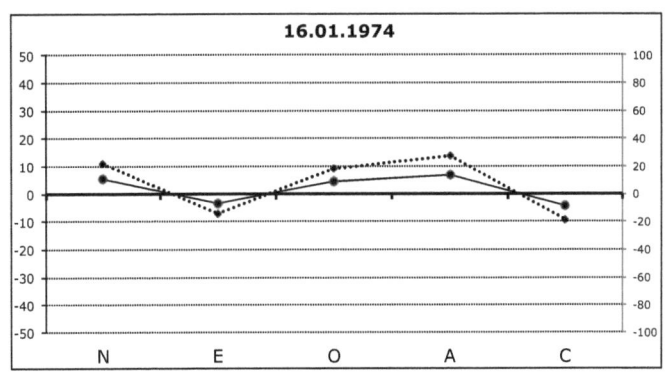

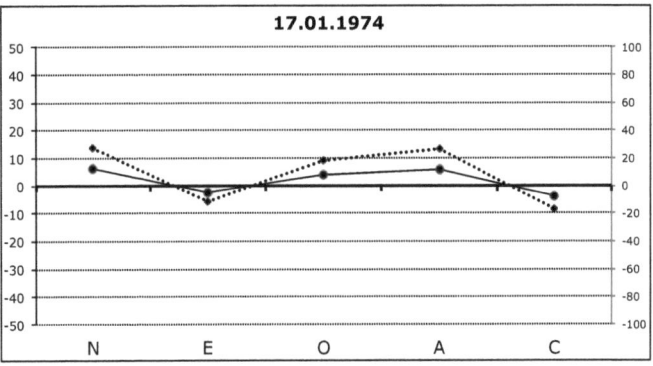

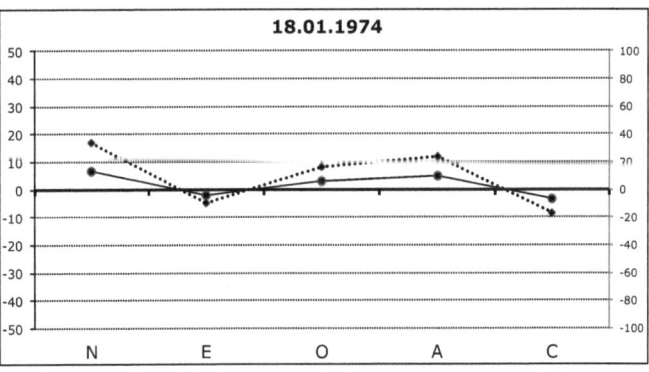

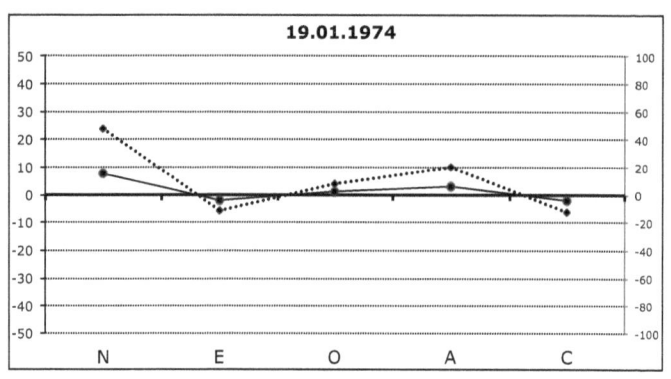

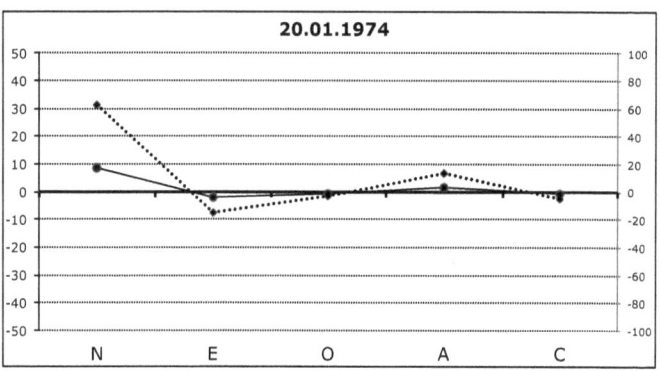

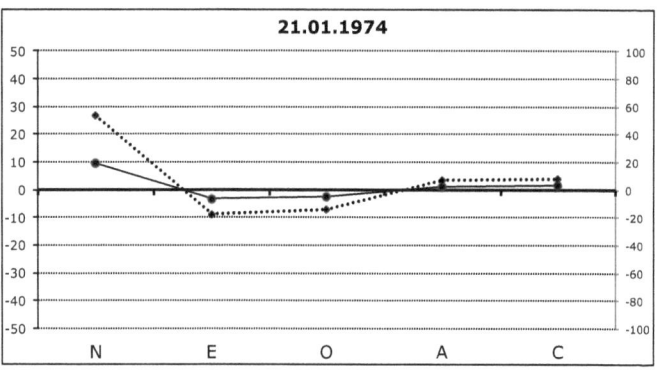

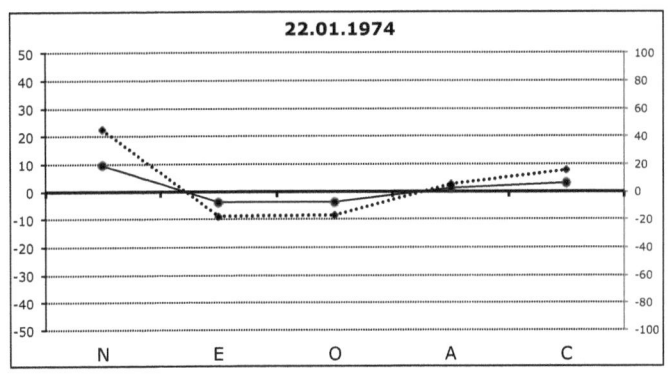

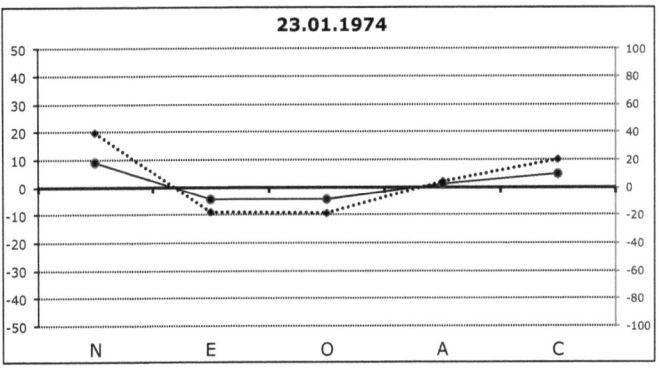

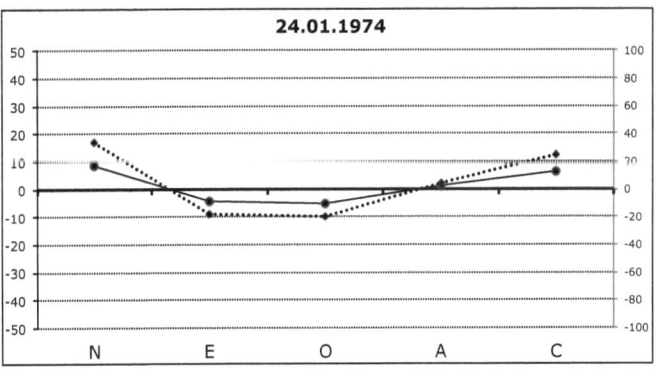

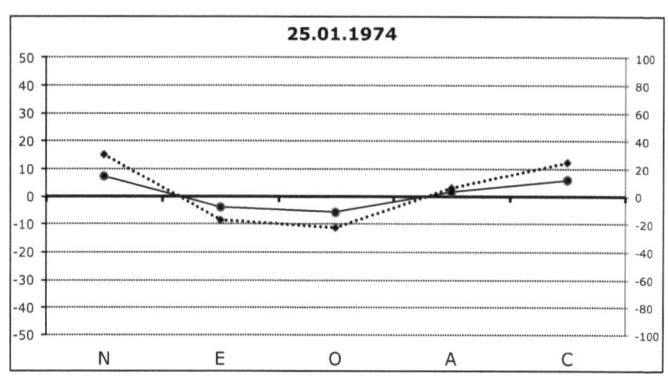

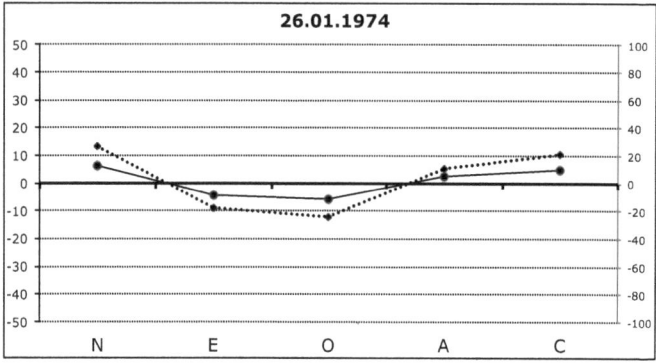

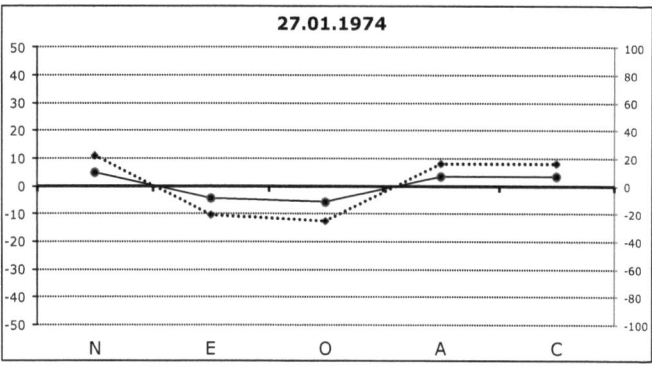

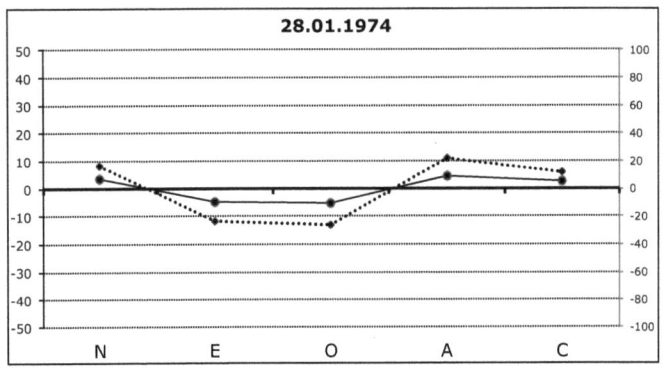

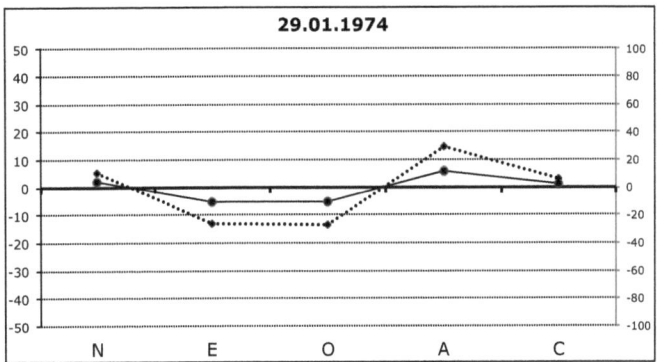

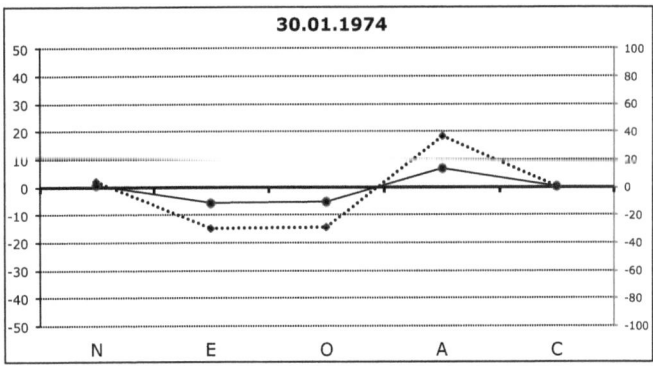

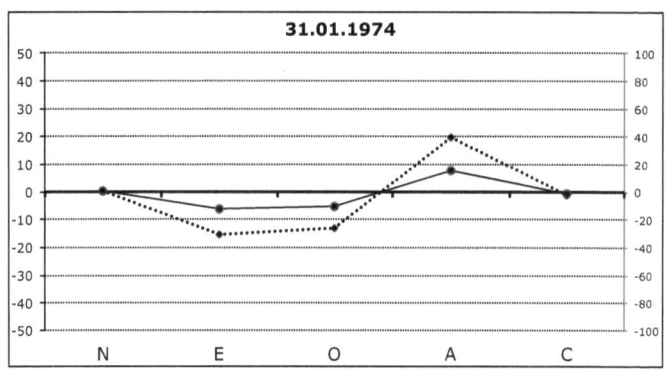

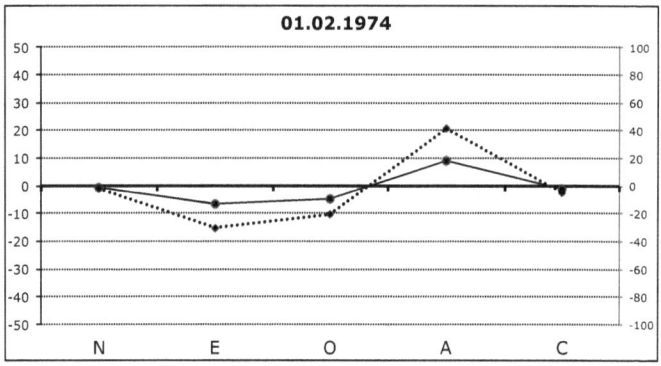

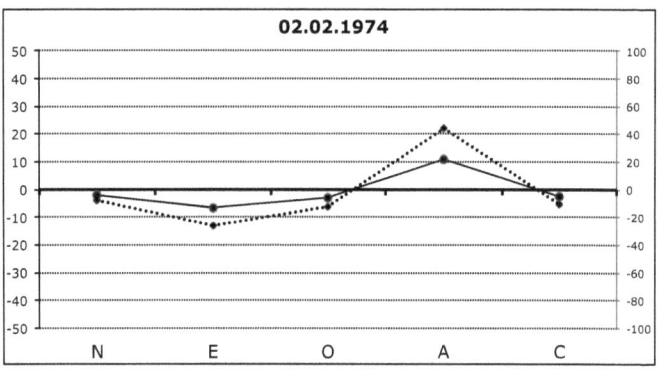

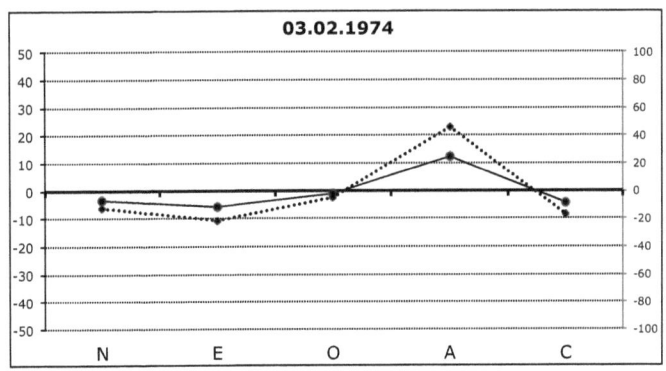

03.02.1974

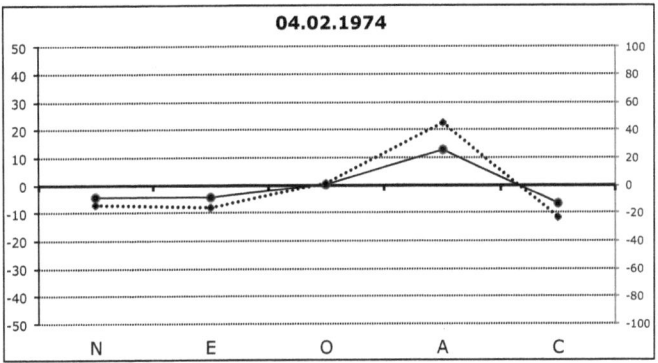

04.02.1974

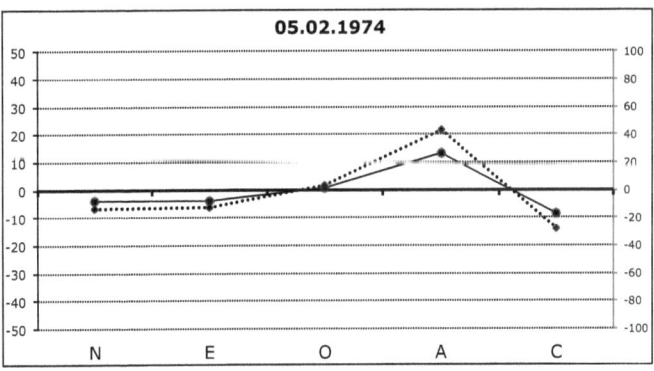

05.02.1974

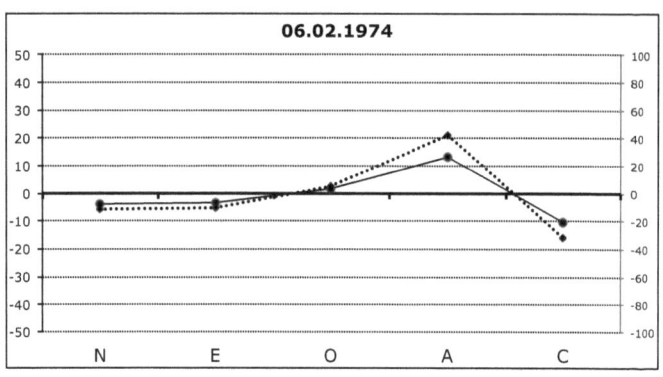

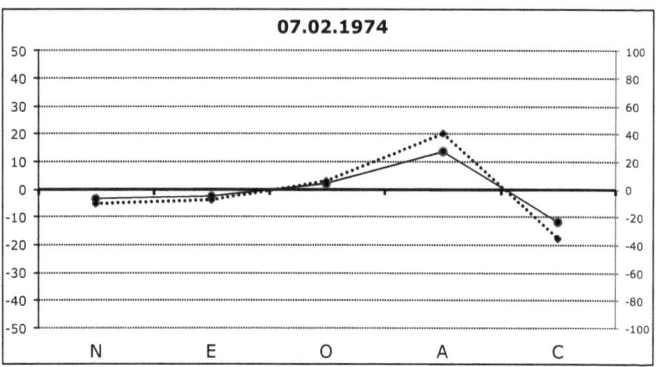

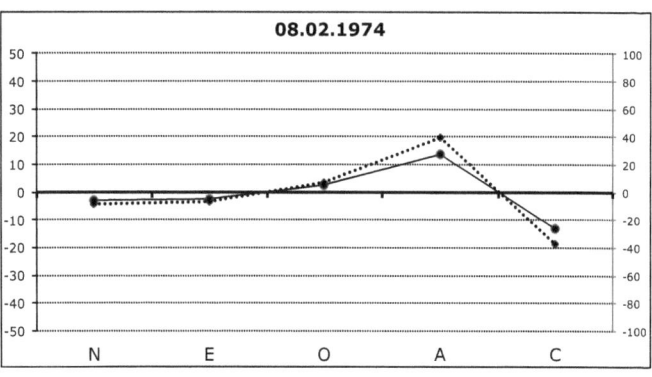

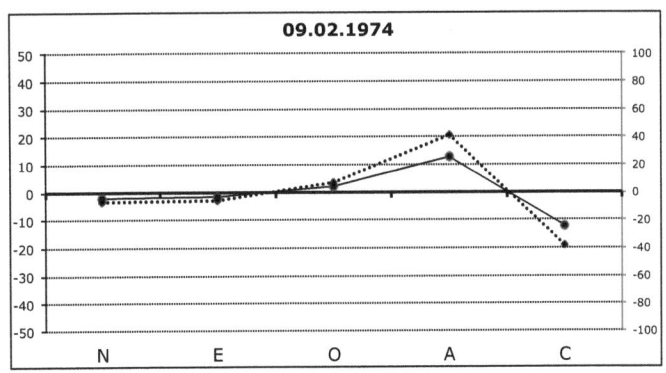

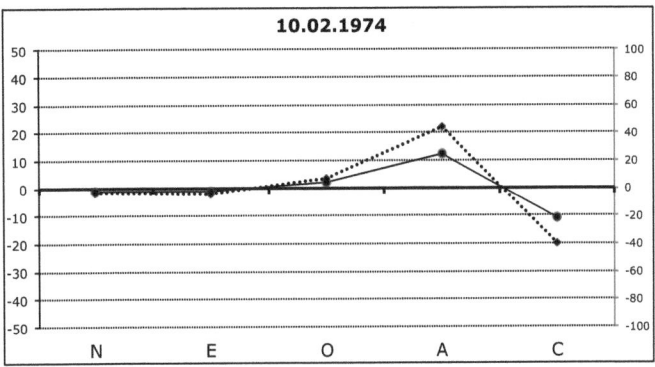

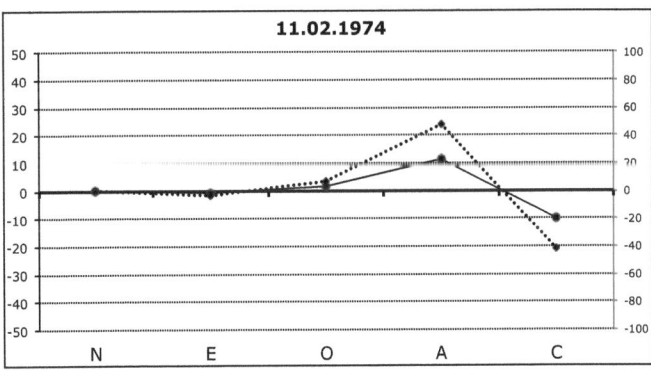

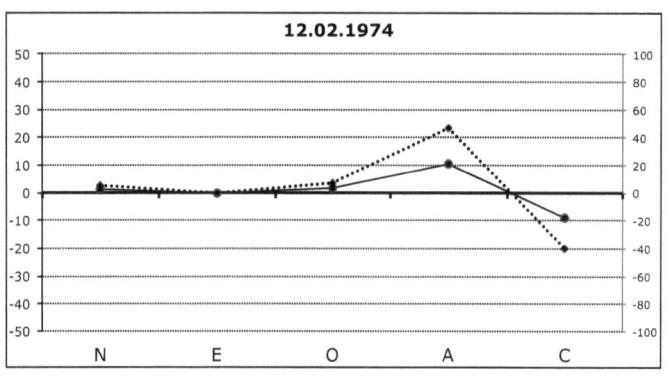

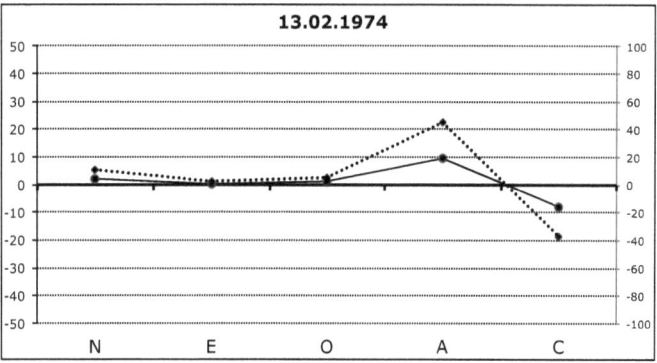

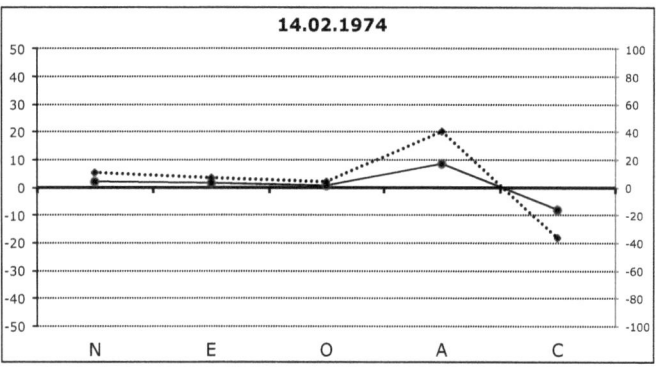

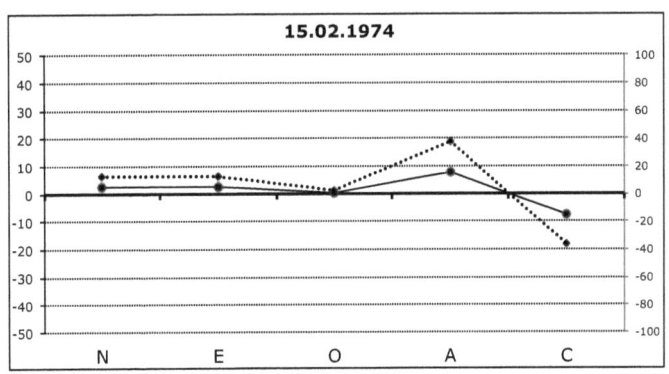

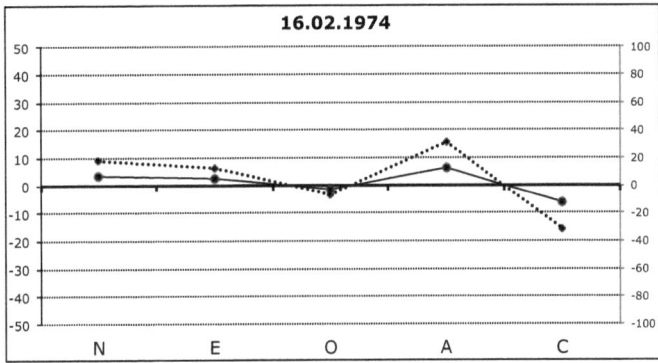

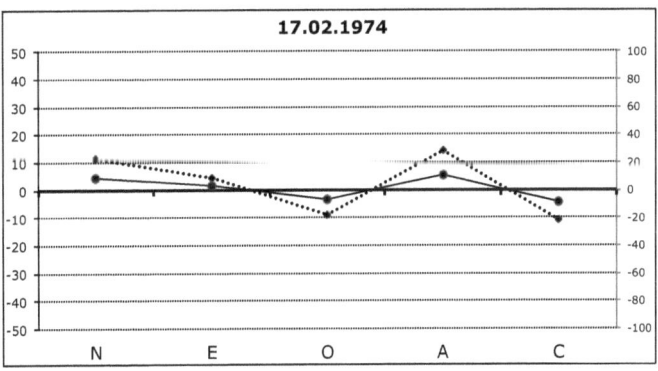

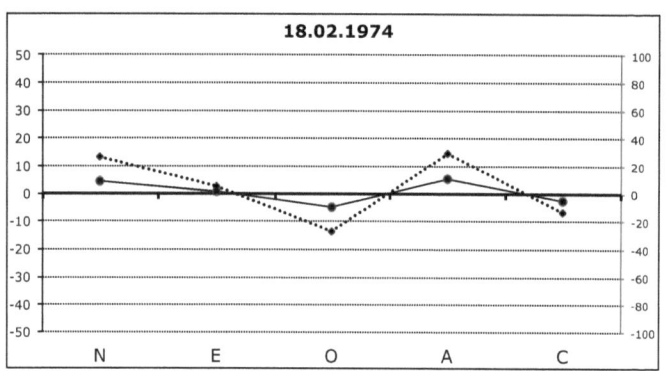

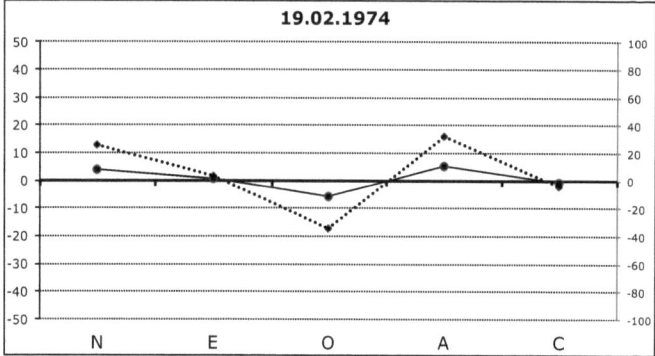

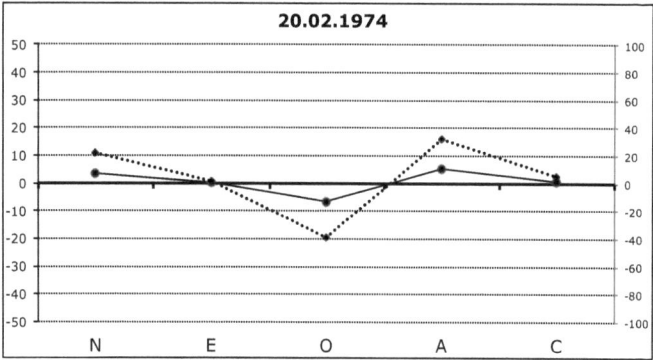

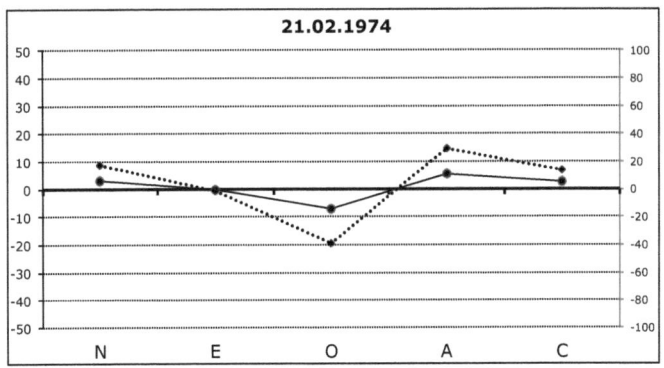

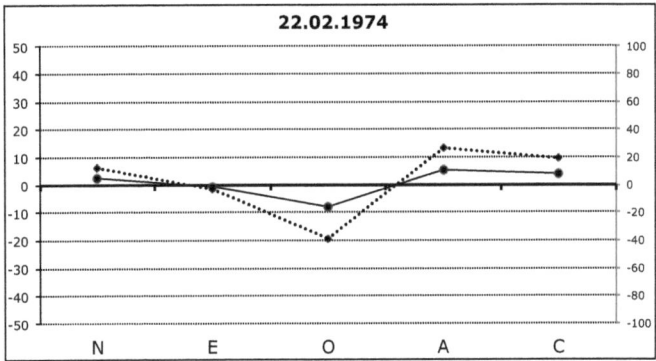

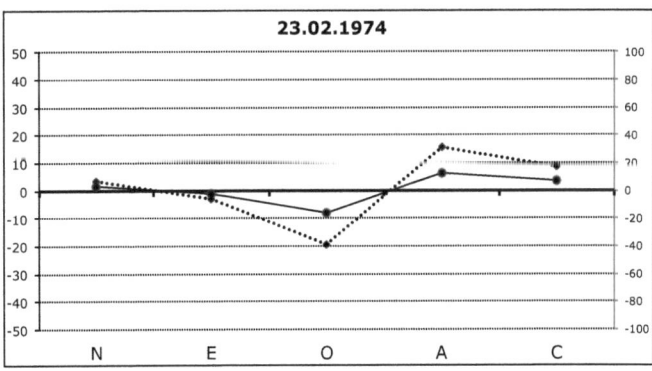

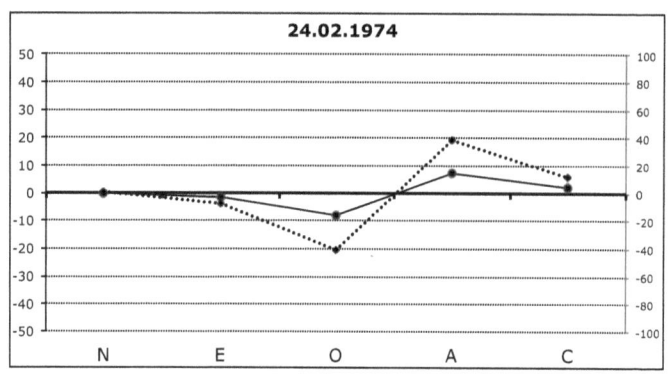

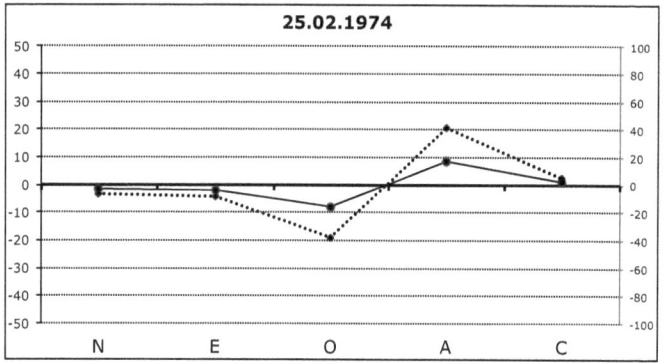

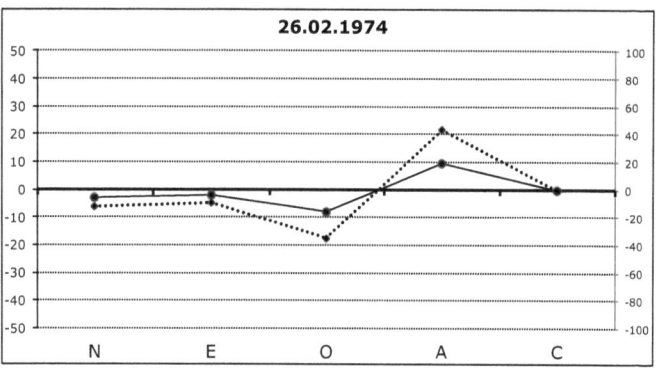

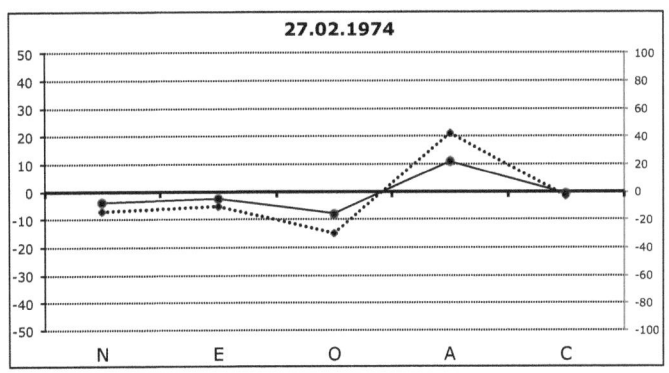

27.02.1974

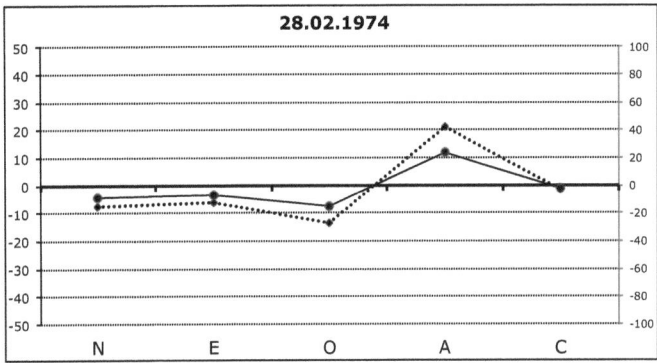

28.02.1974

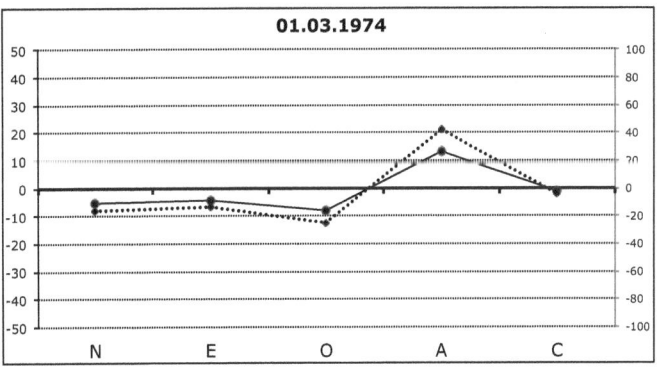

01.03.1974

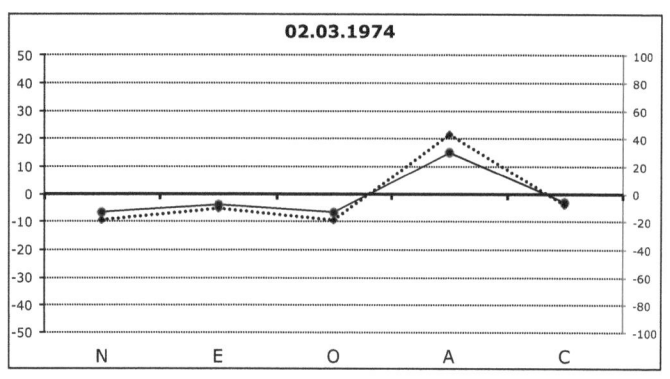

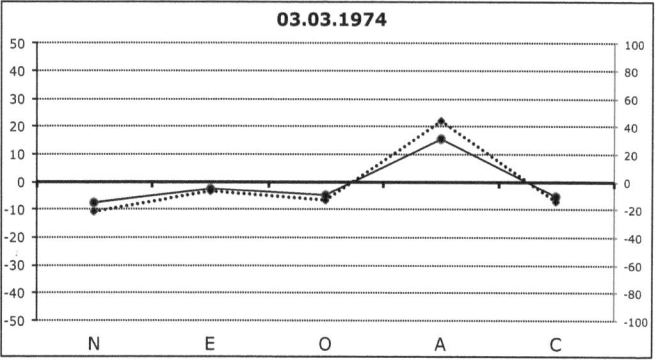

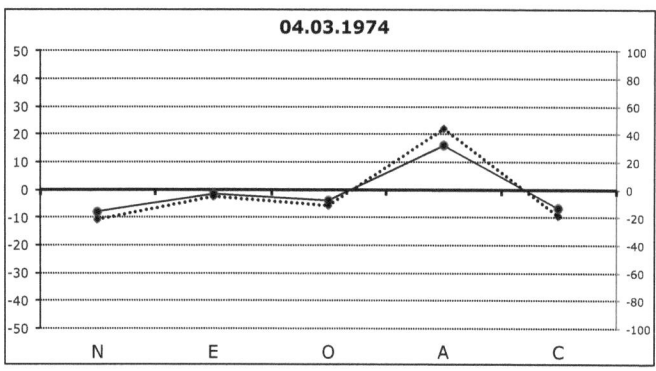

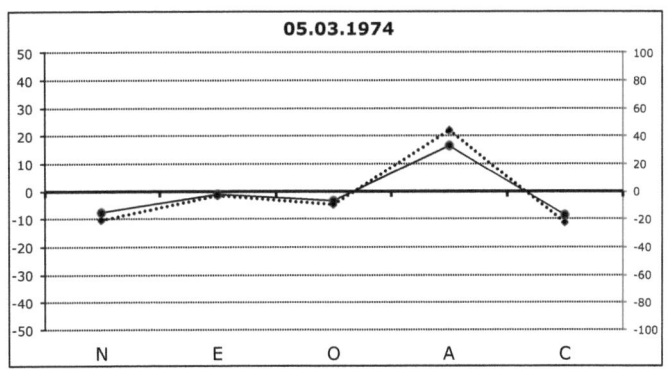

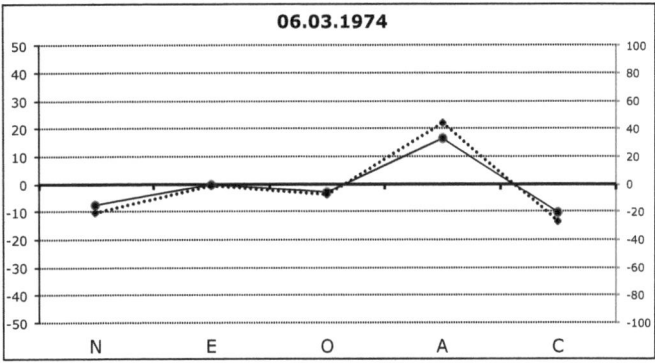

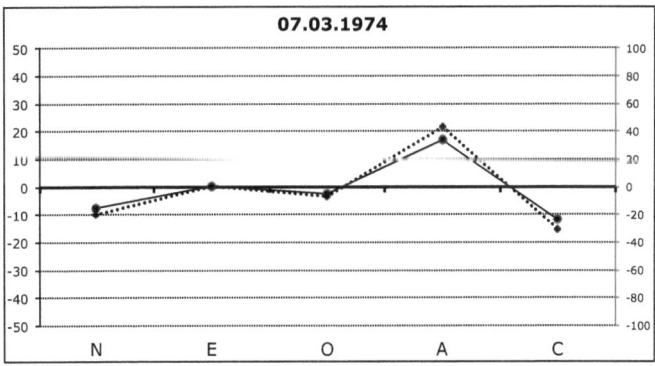

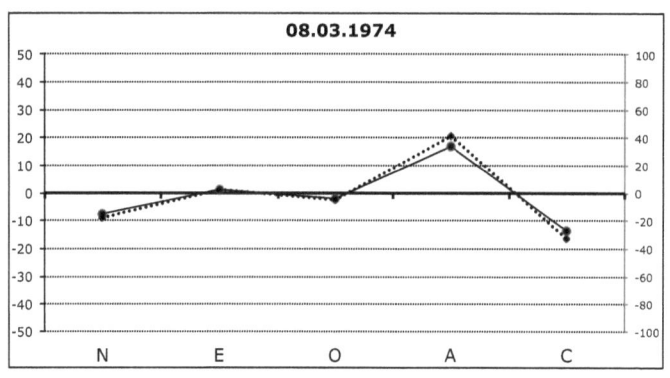

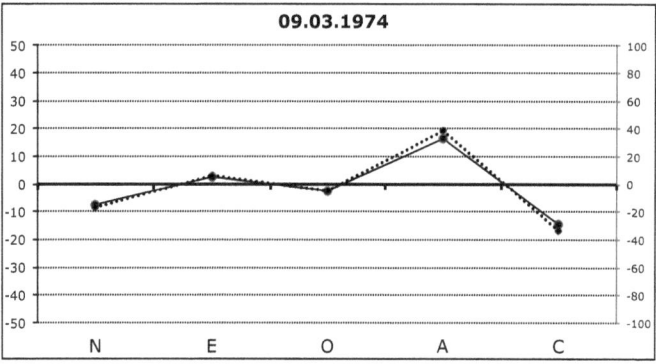

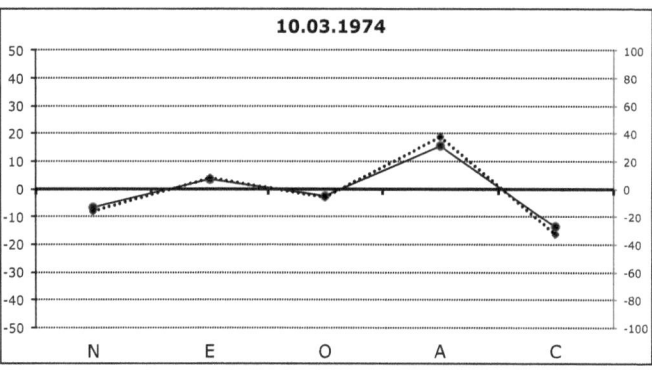

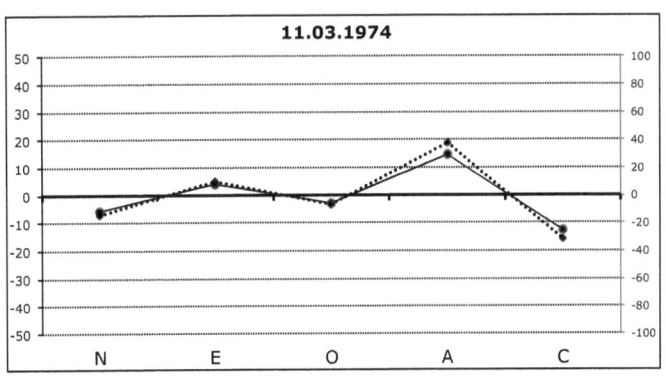

11.03.1974

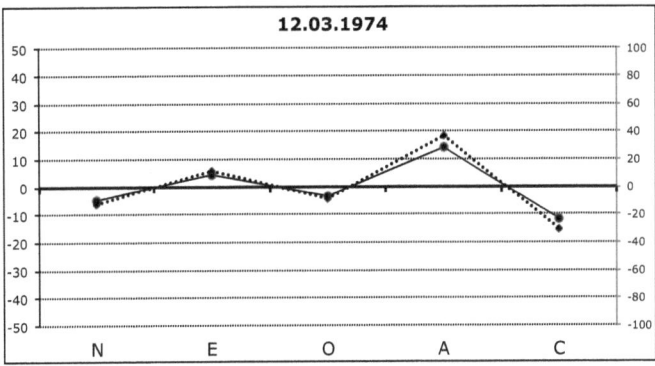

12.03.1974

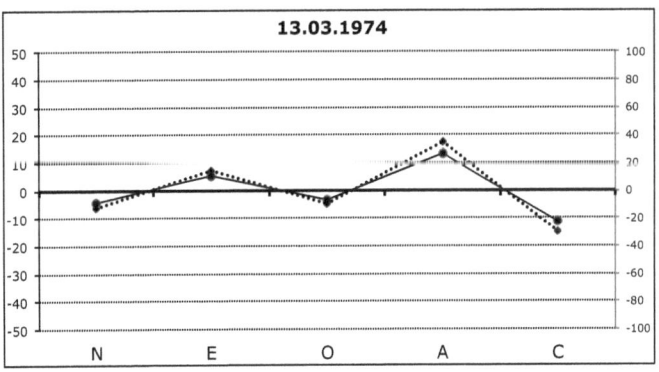

13.03.1974

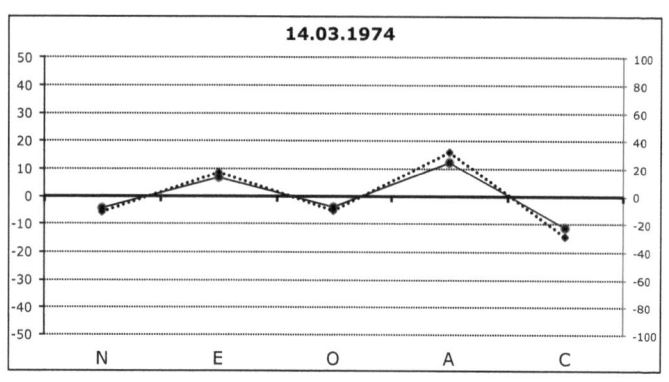

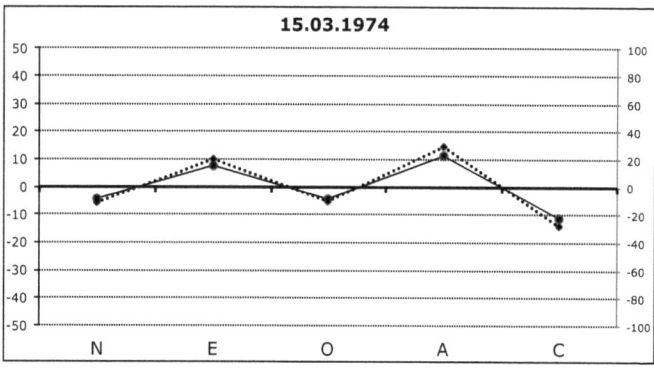

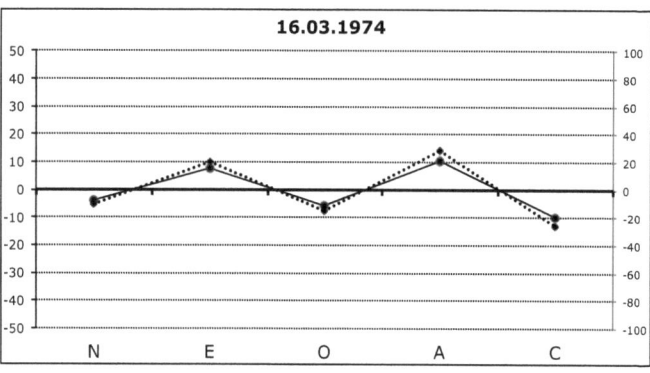

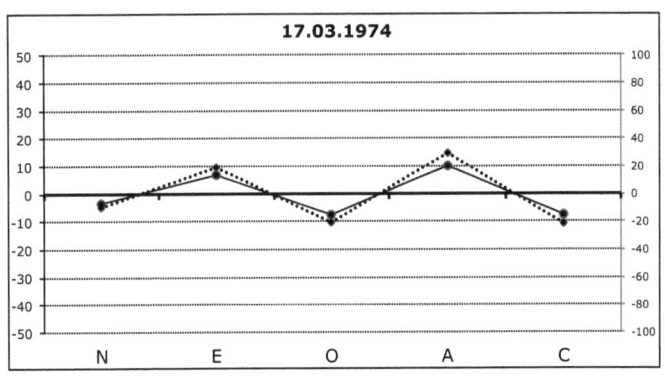

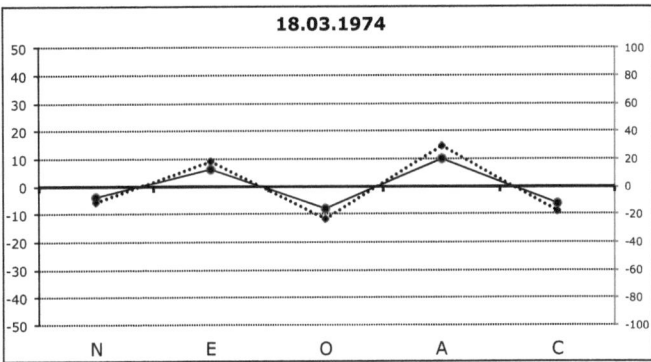

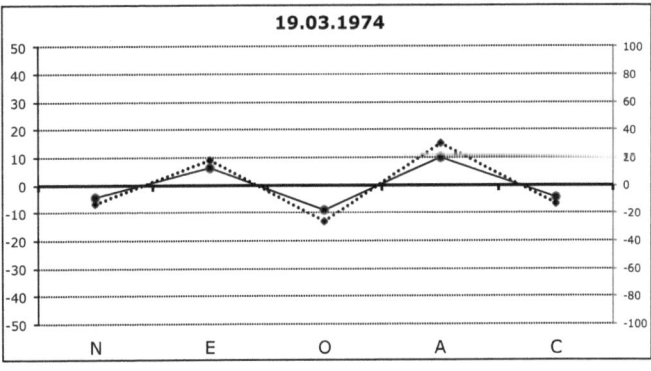

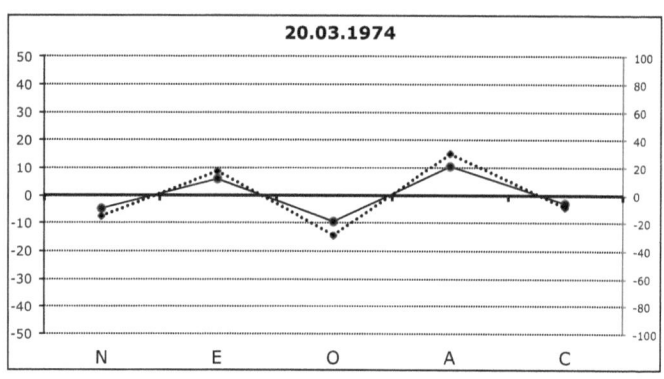

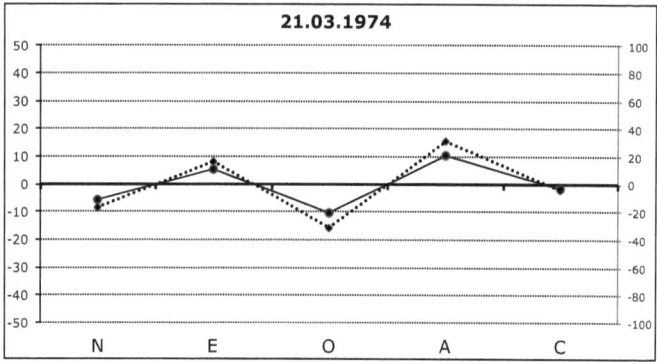

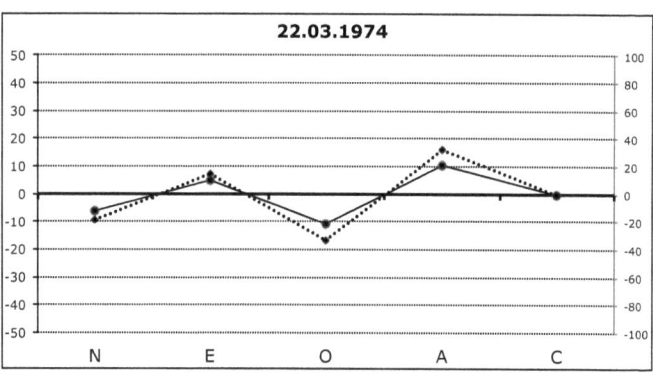

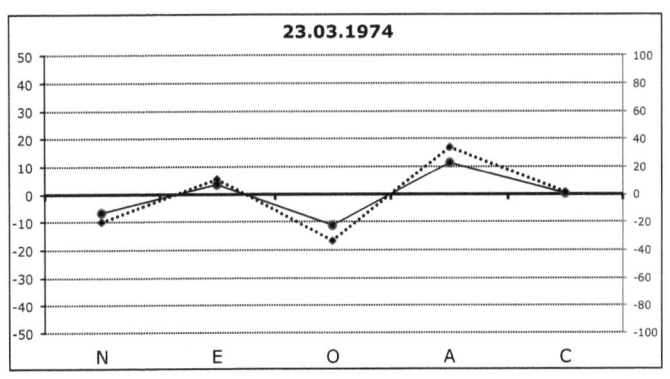

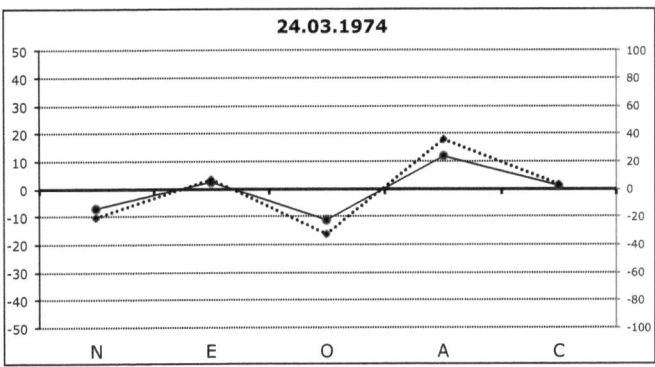

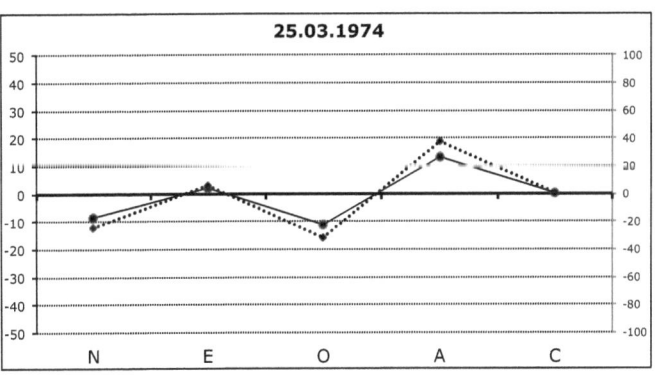

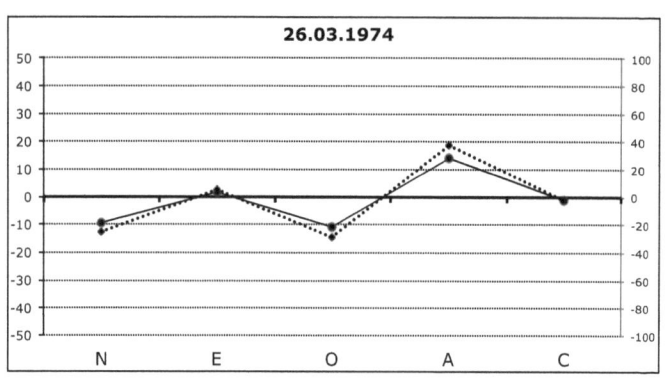

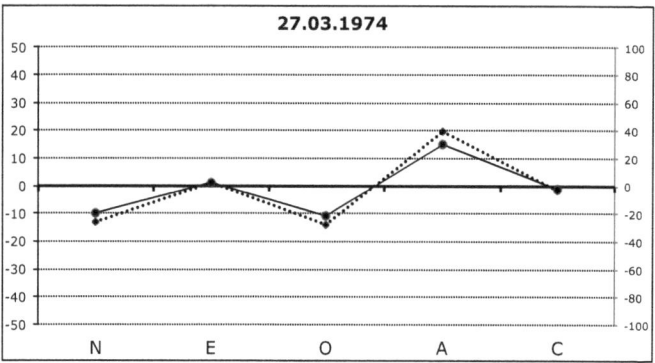

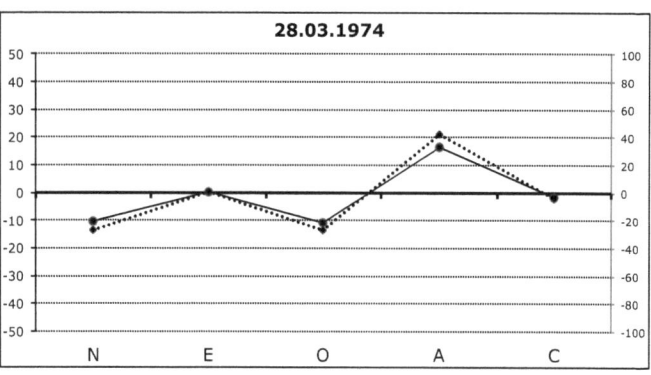

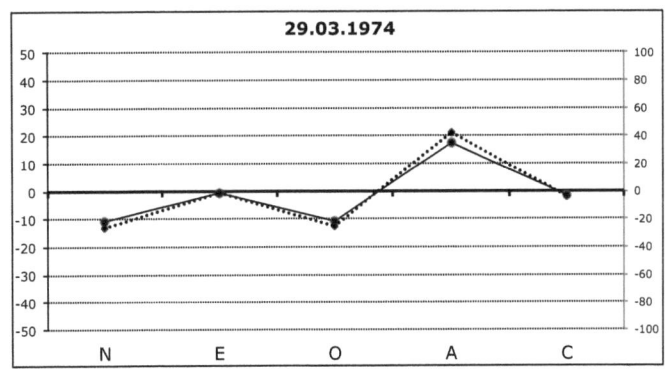

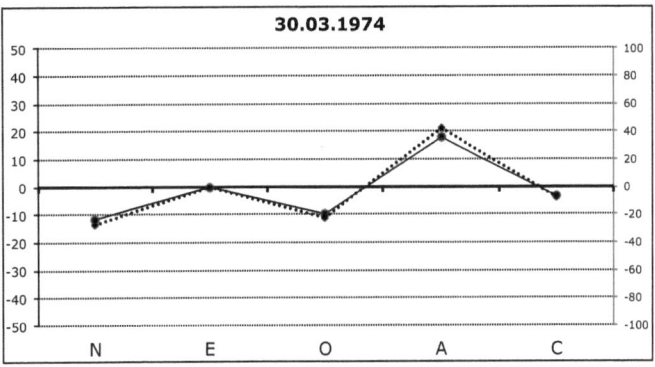

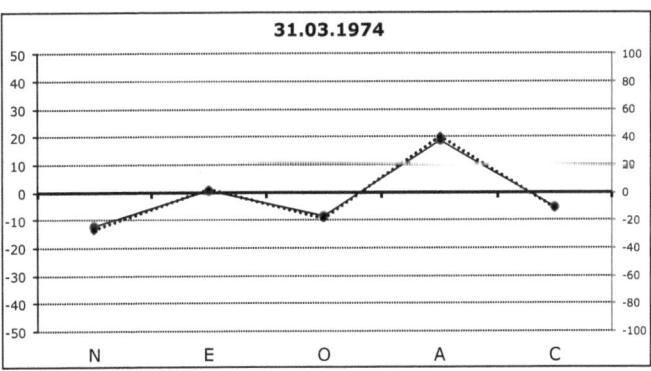

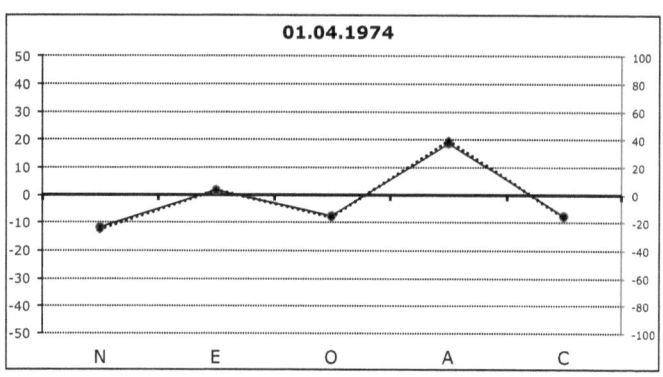

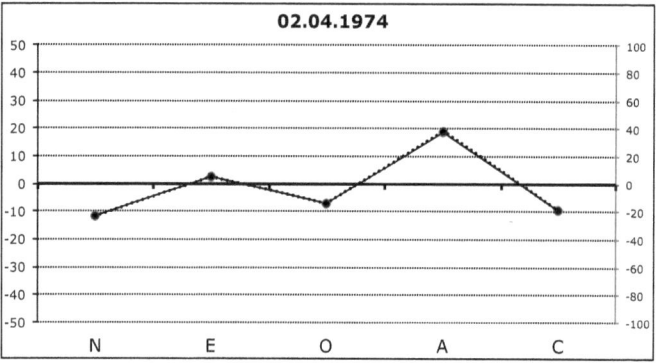

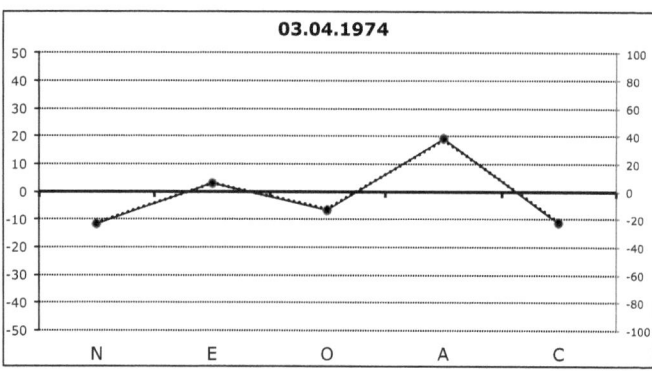

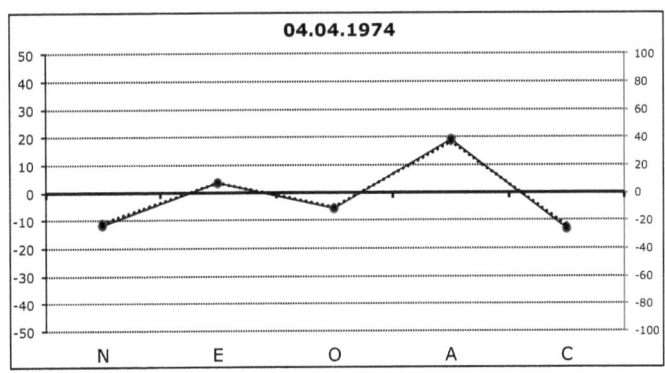

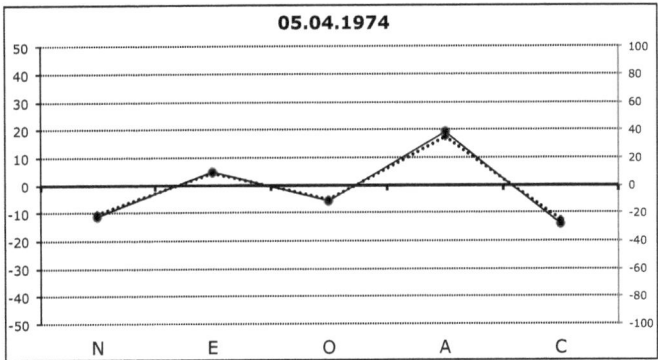

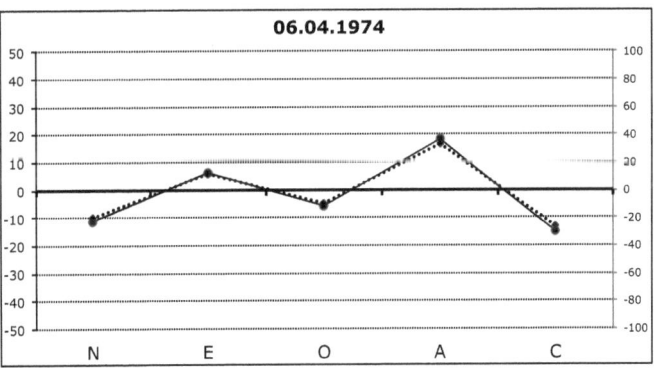

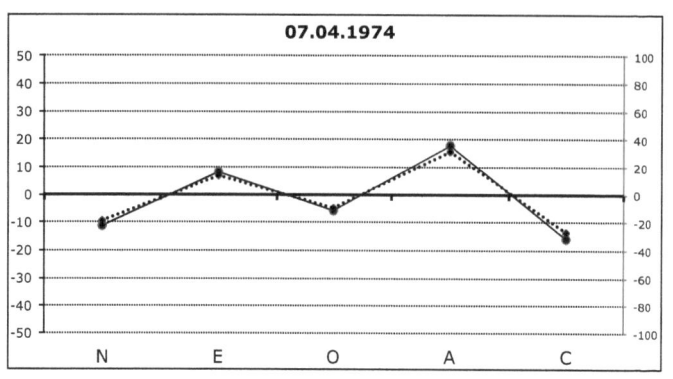

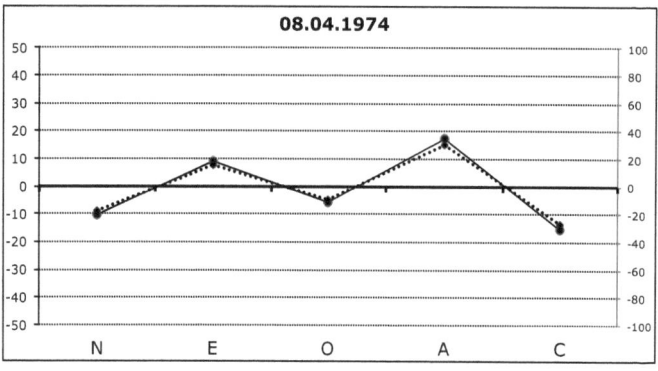

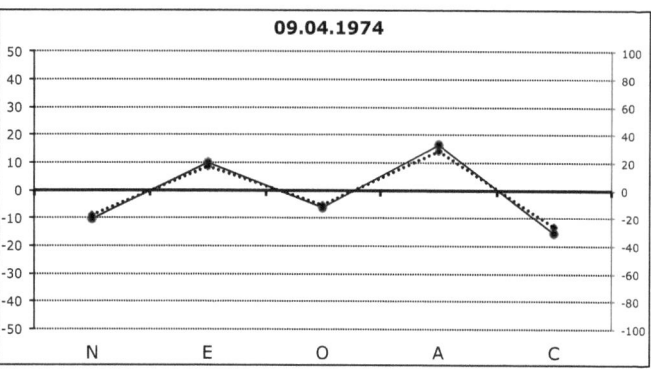

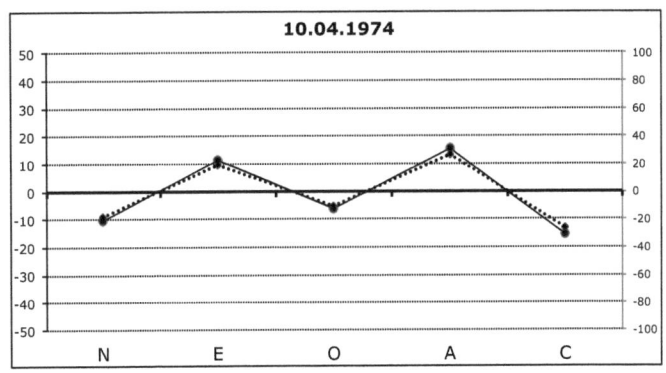

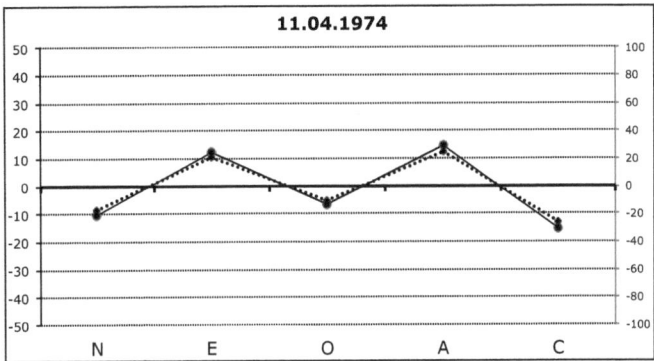

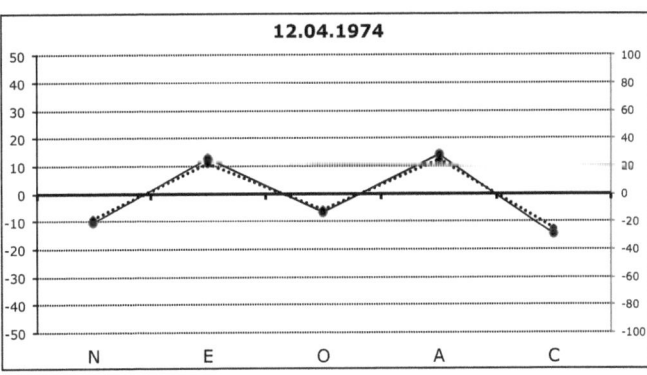

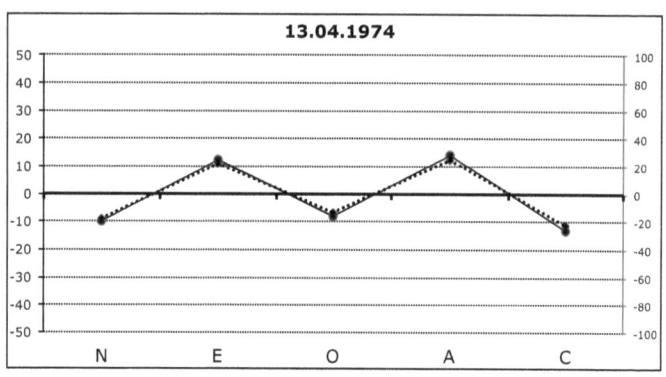

13.04.1974

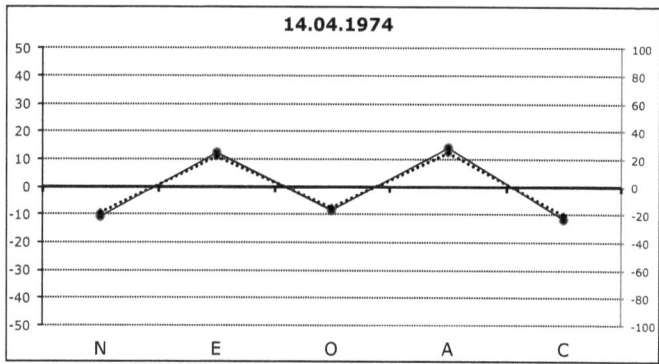

14.04.1974

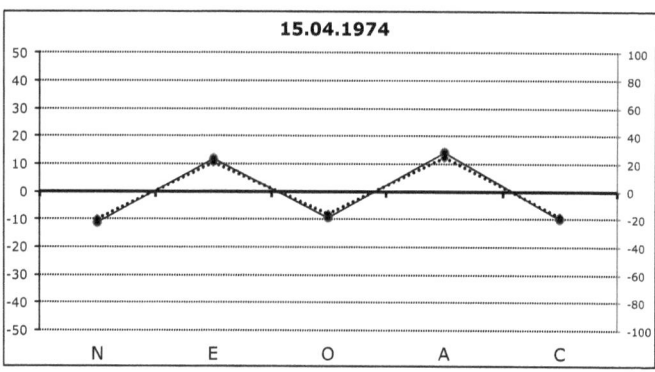

15.04.1974

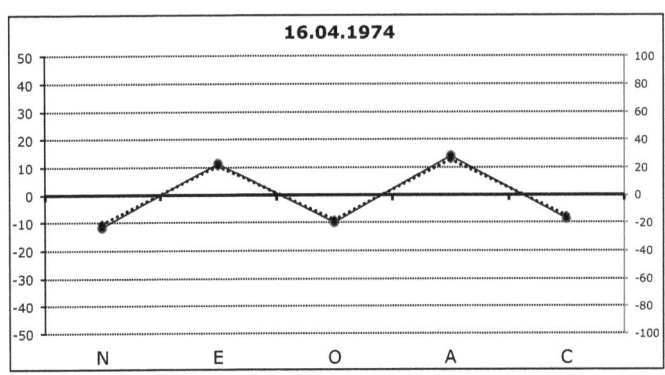

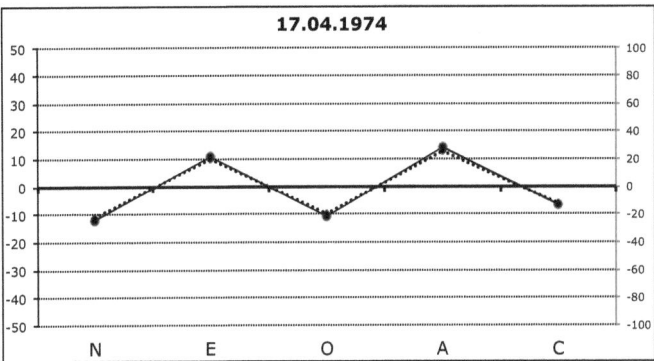

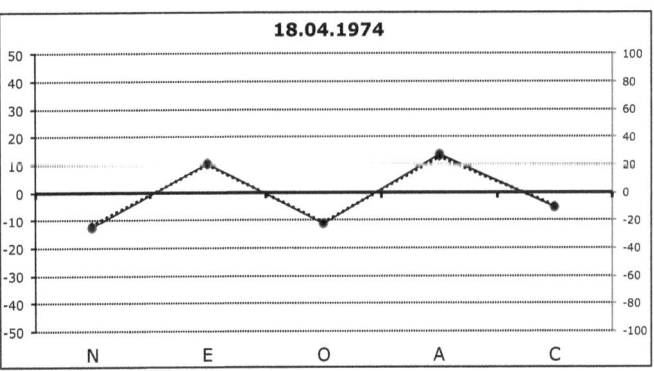

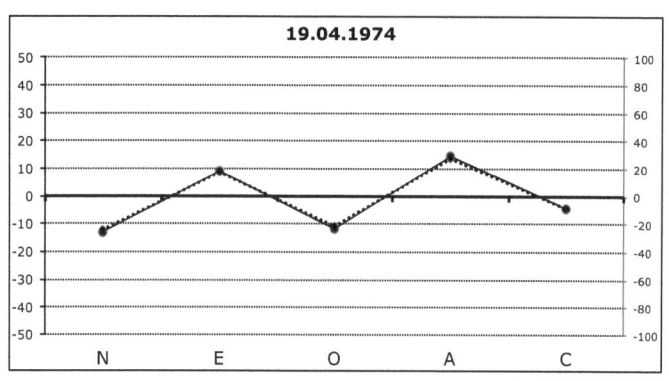

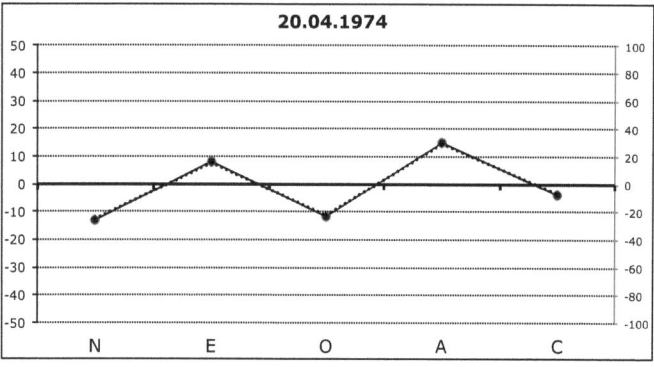

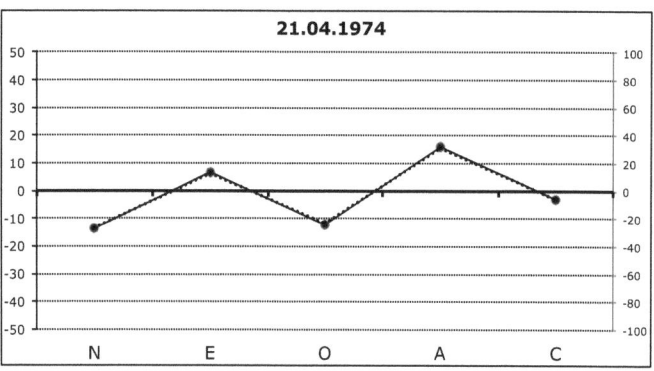

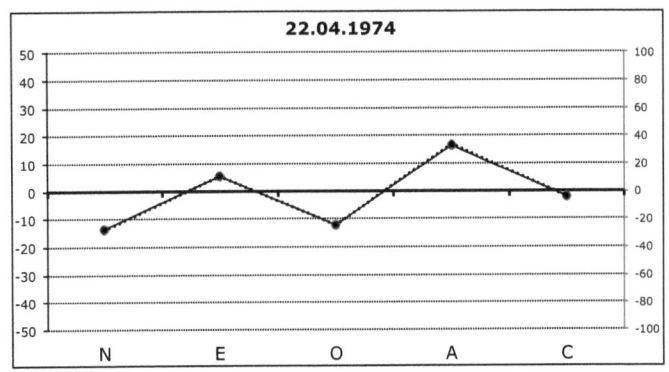

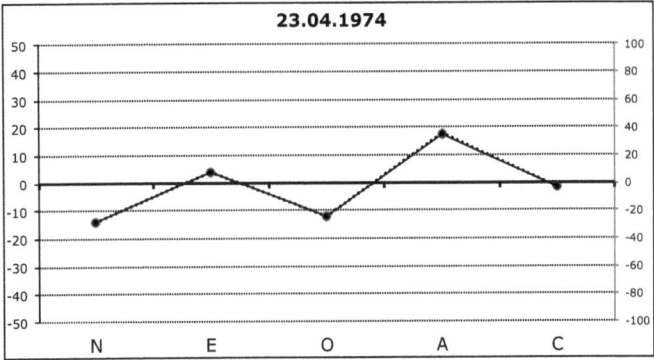

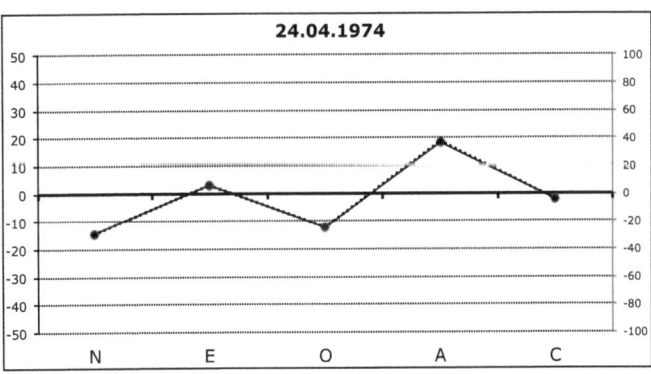

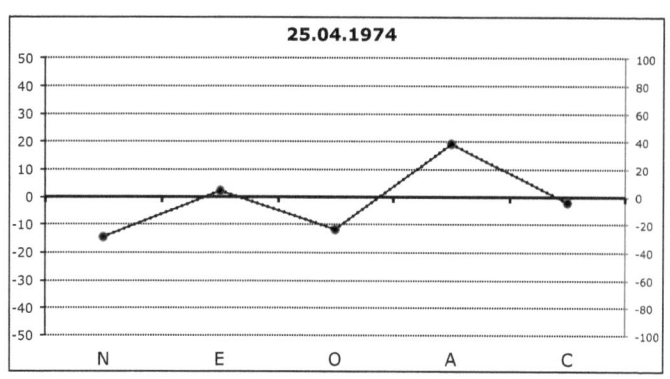

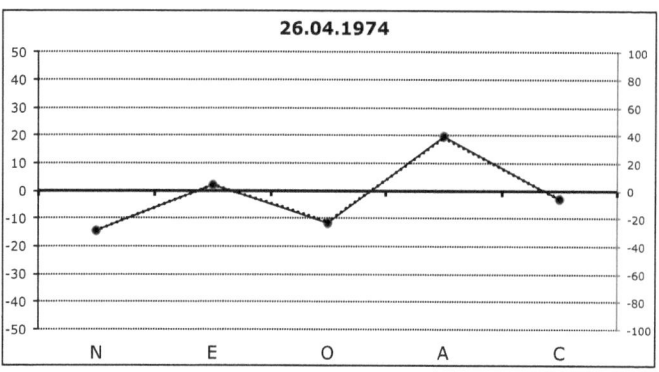

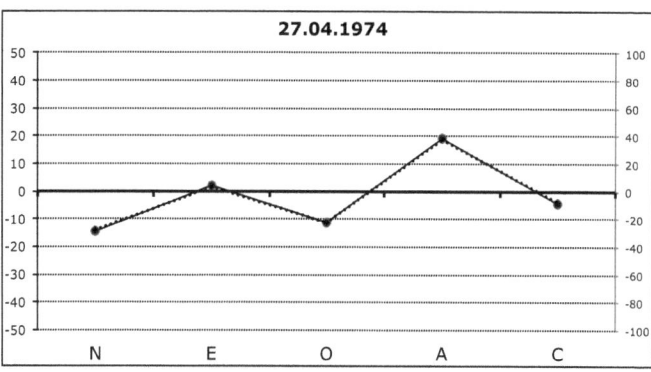

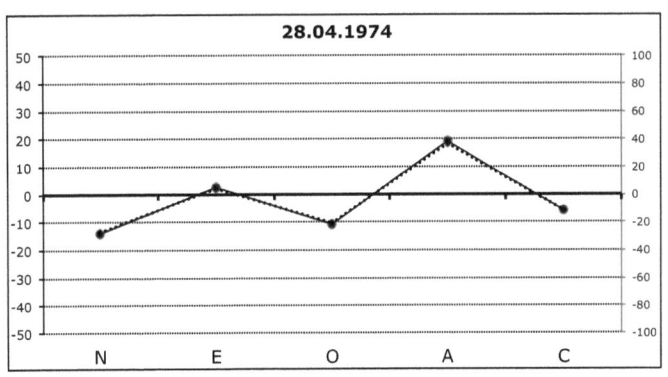

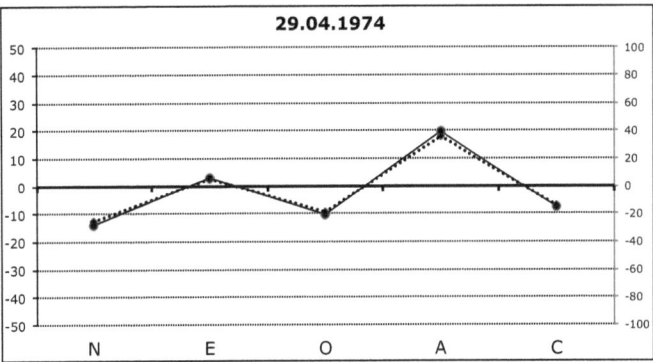

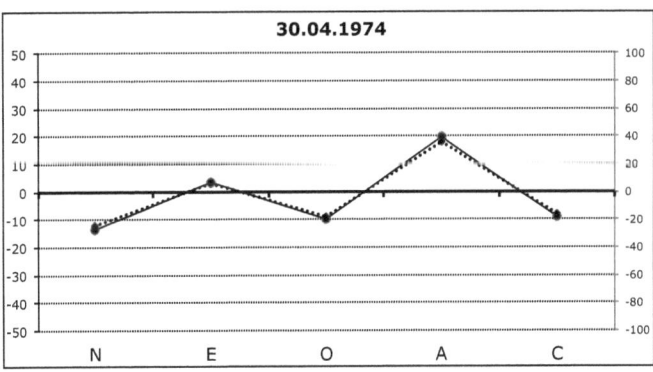

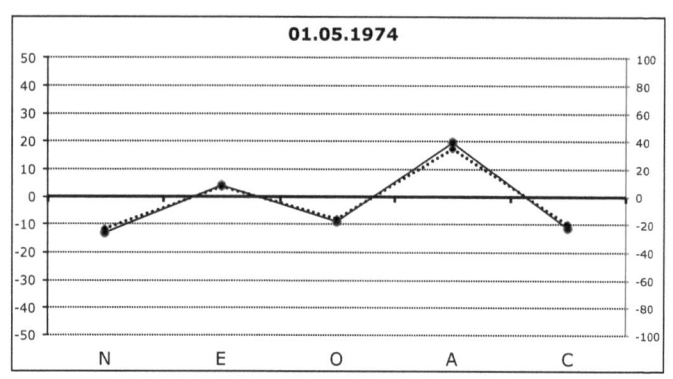

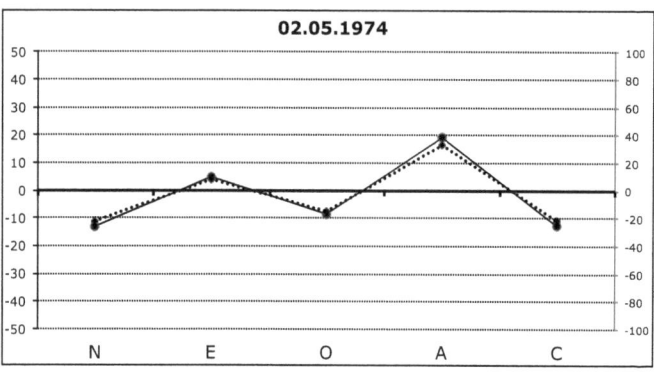

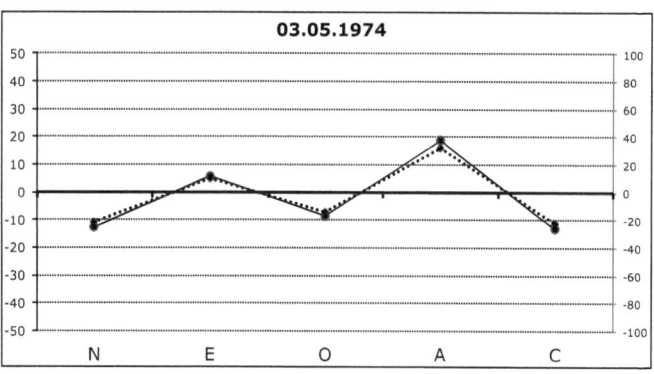

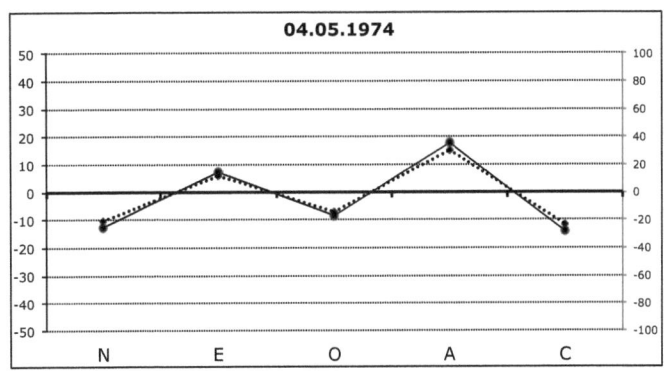

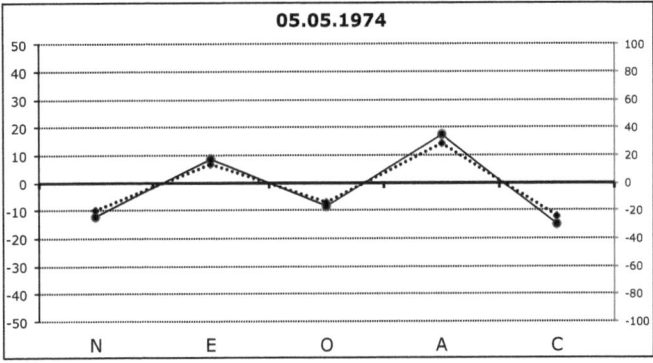

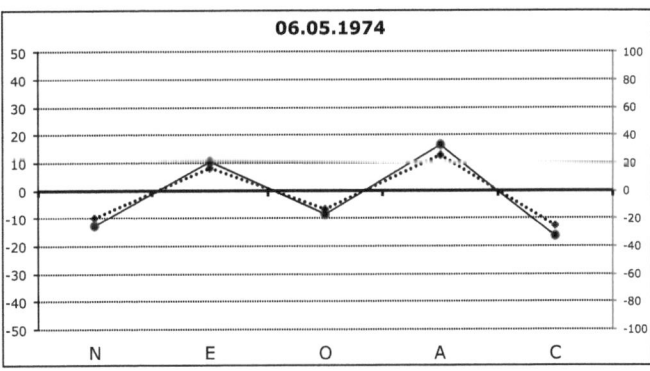

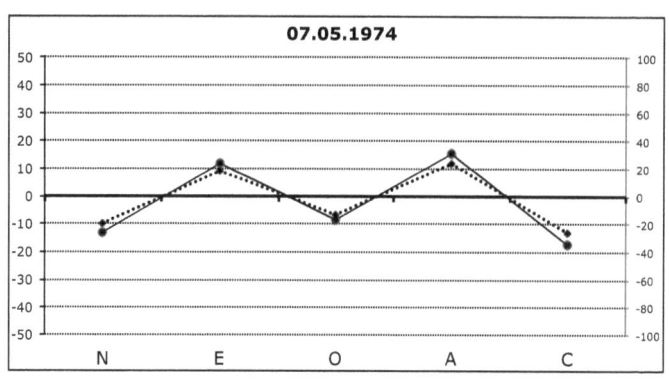

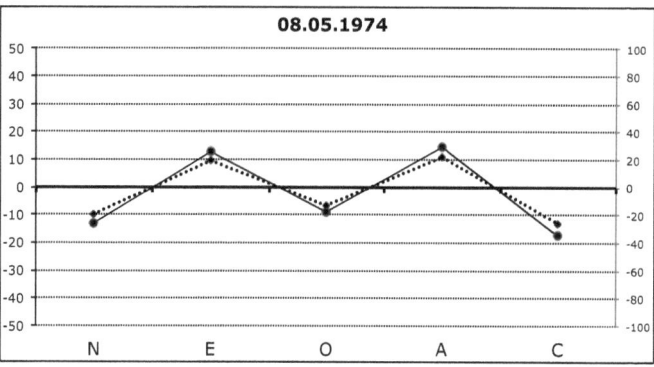

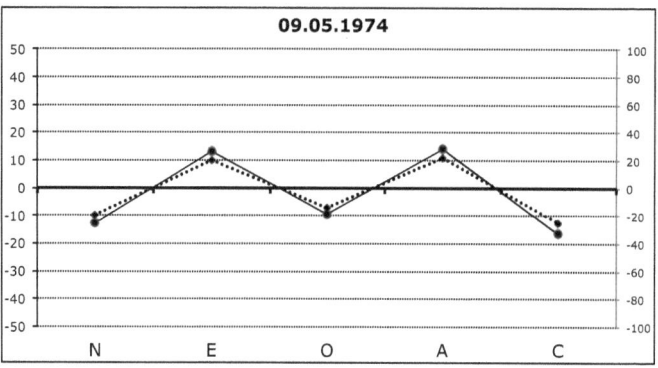

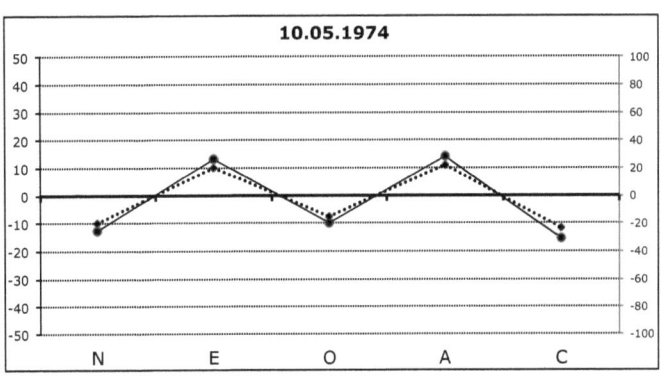

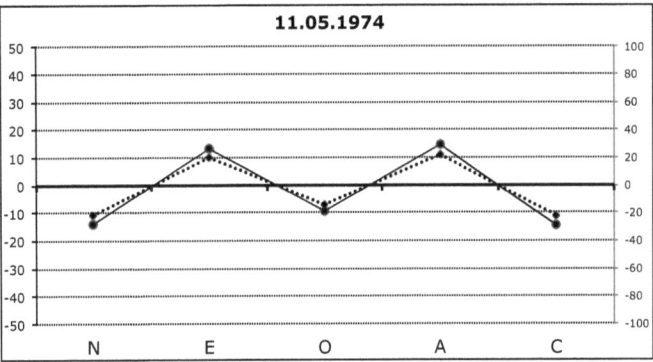

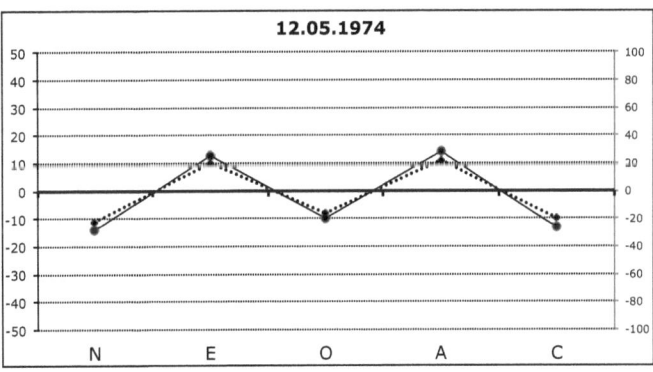

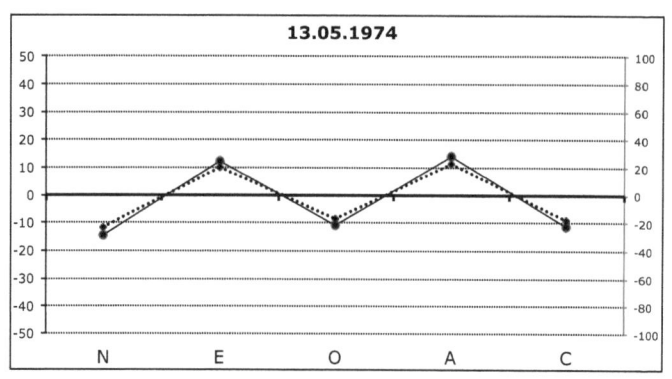

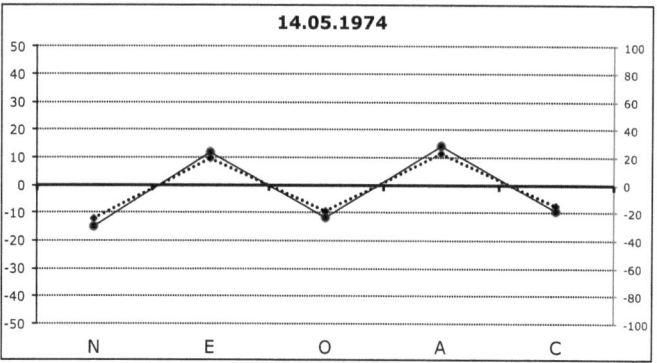

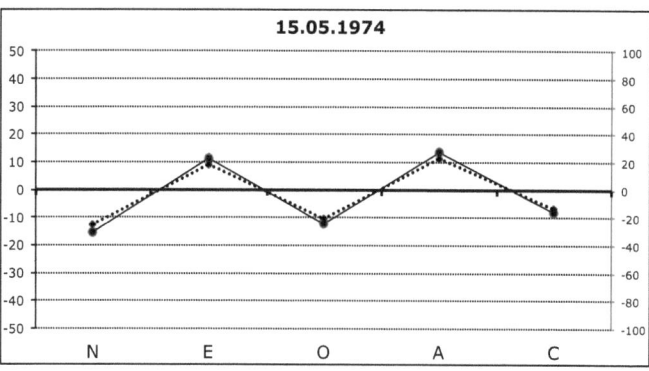

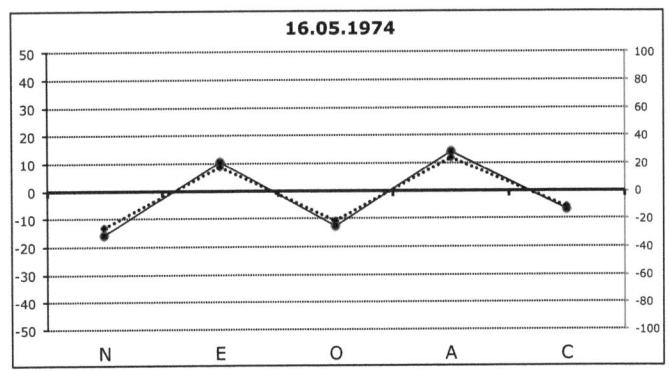

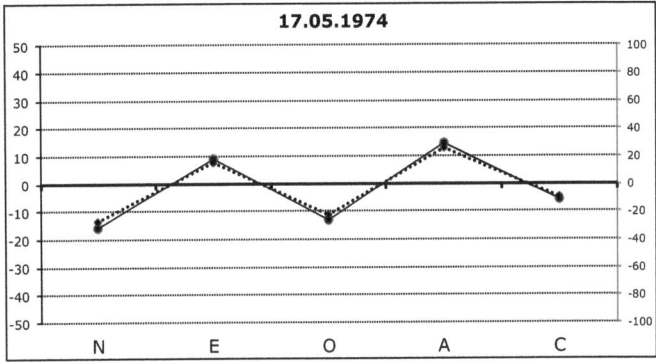

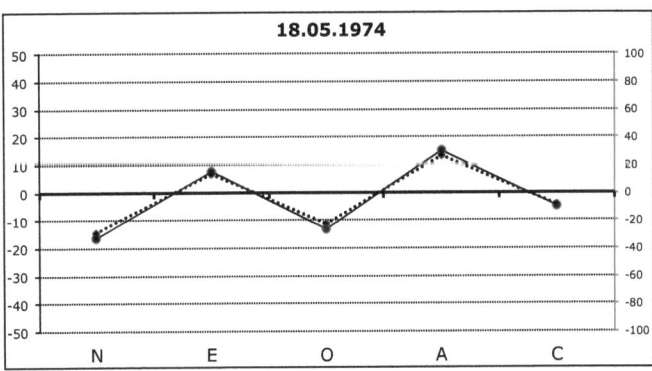

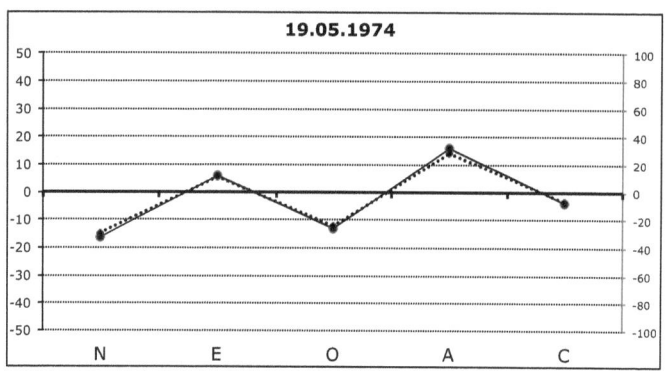

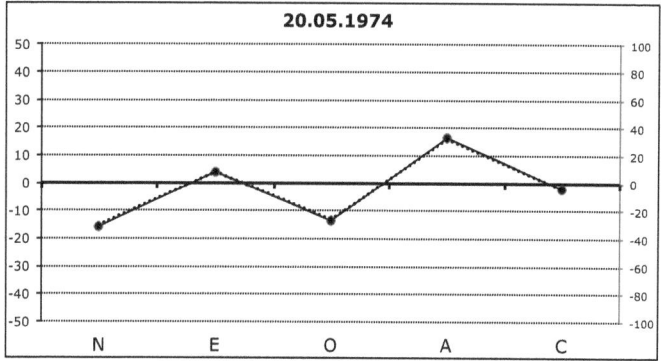

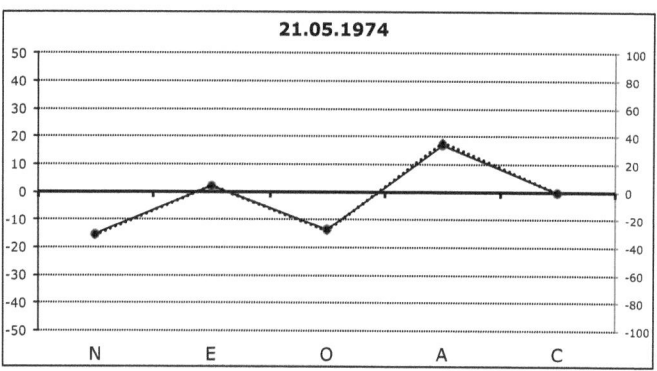

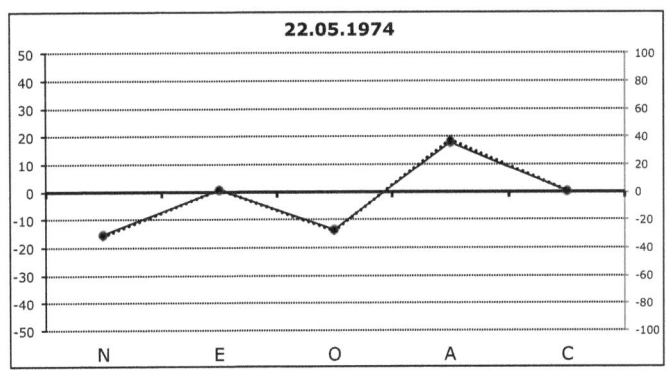

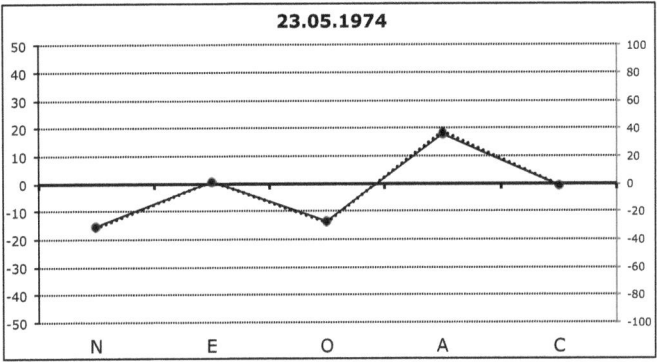

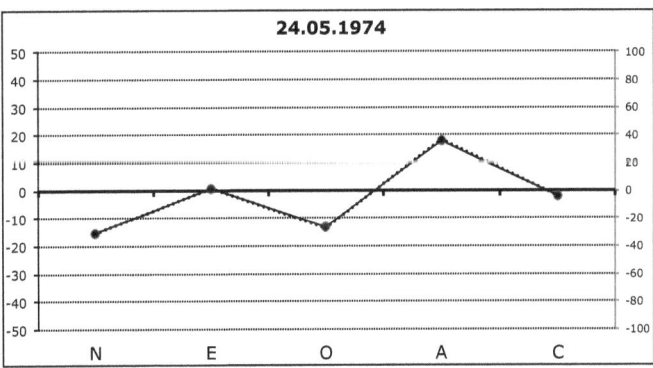

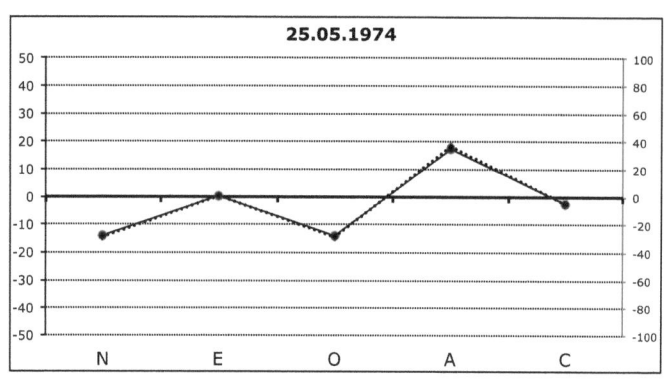

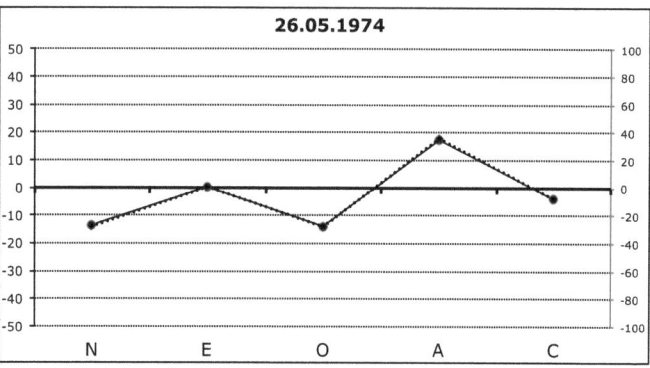

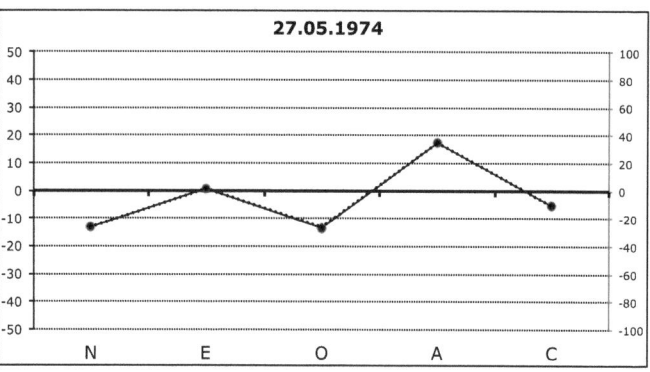

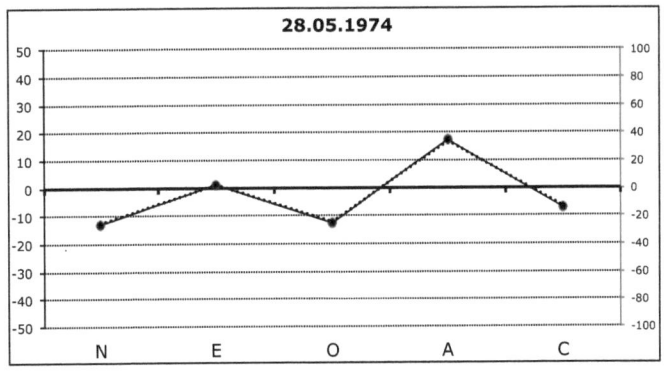

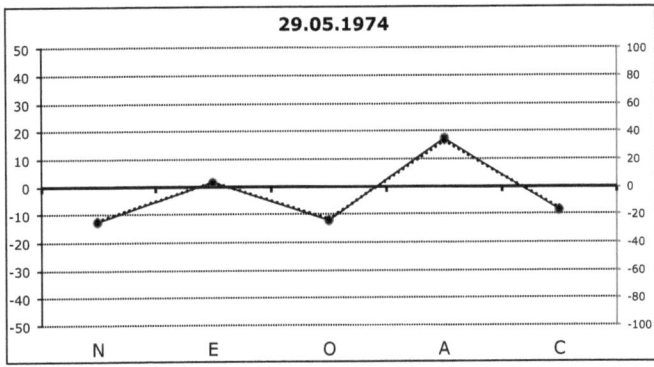

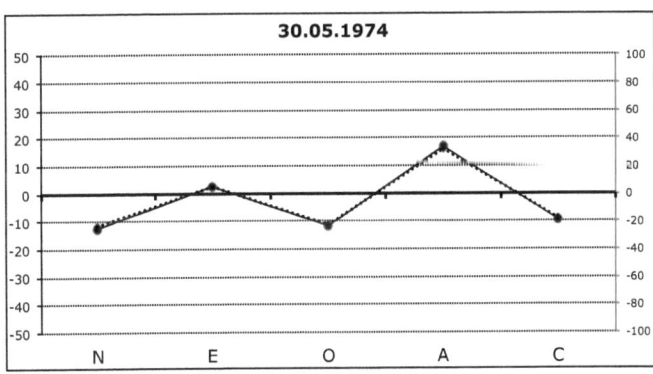

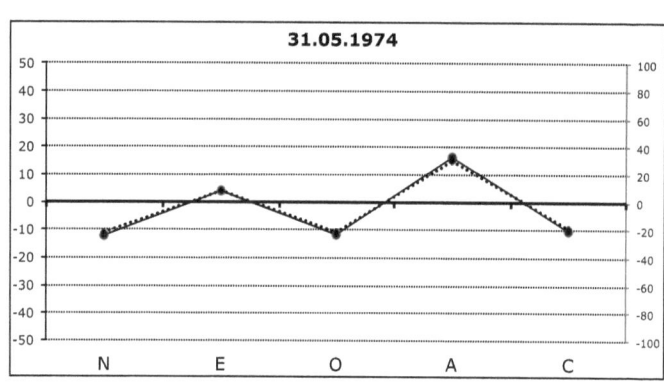

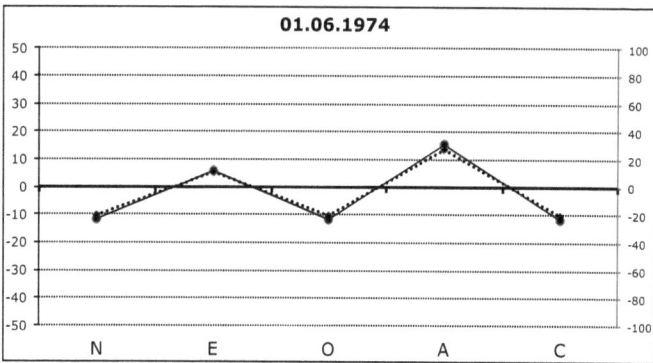

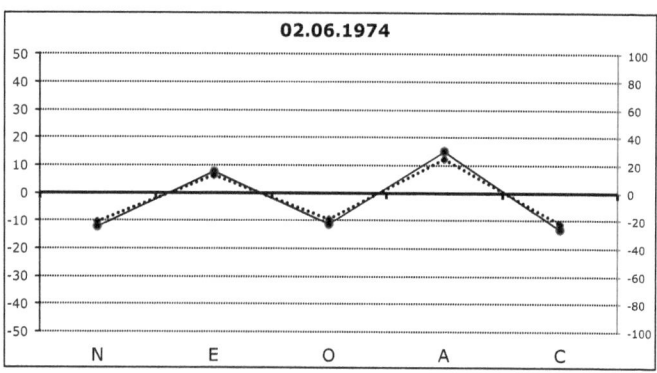

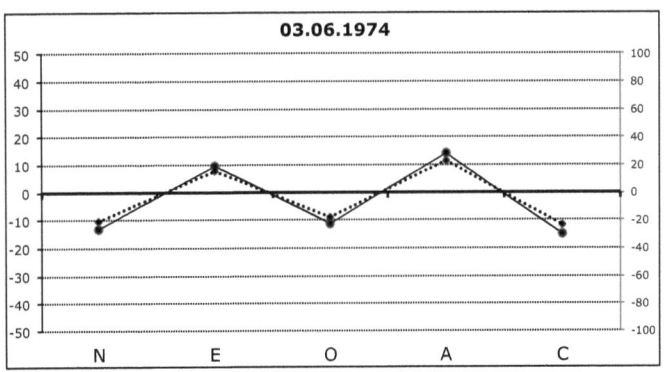

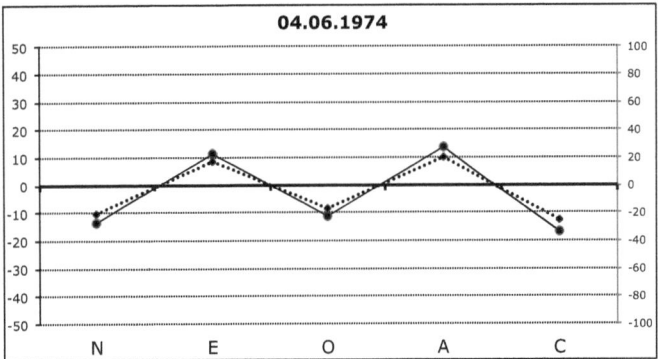

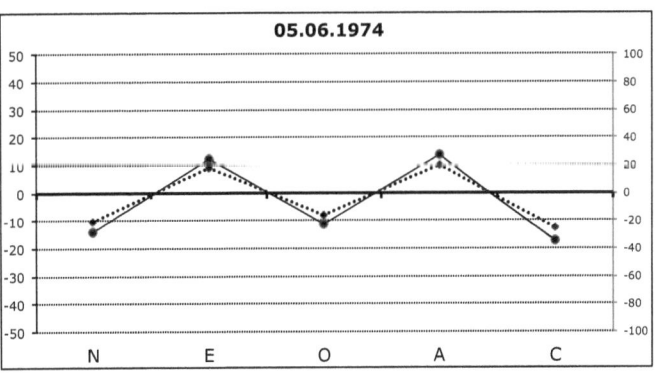

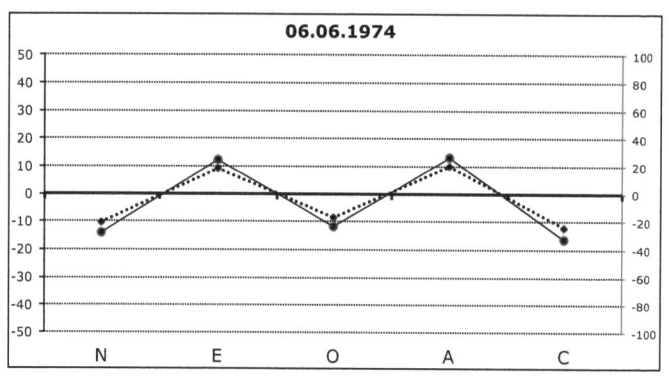

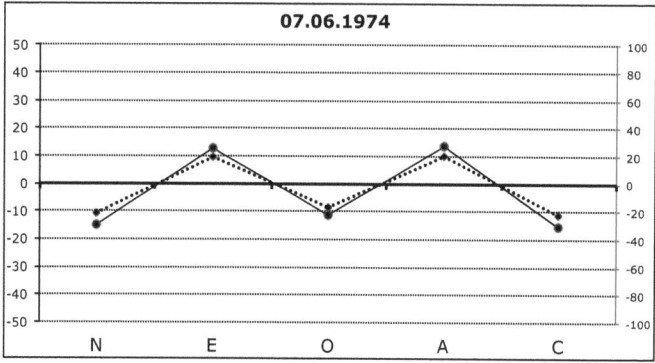

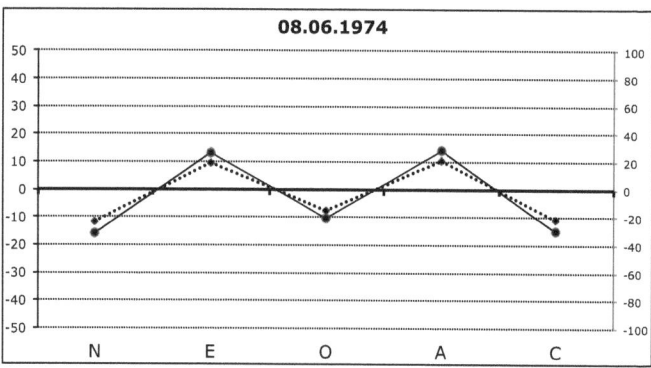

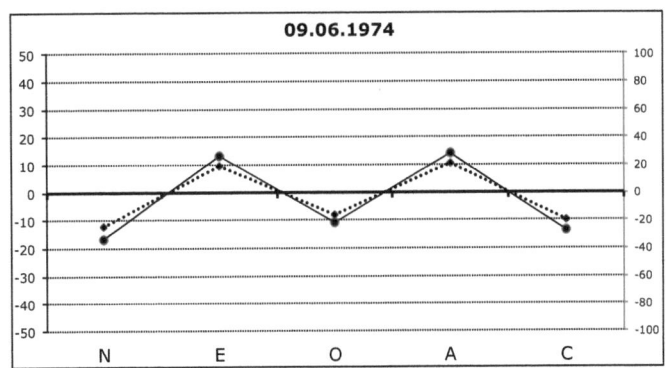

09.06.1974

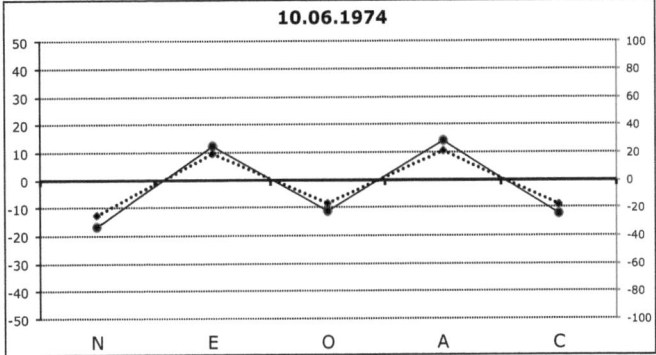

10.06.1974

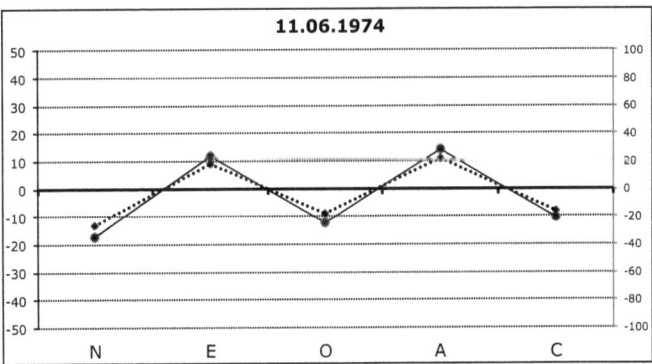

11.06.1974

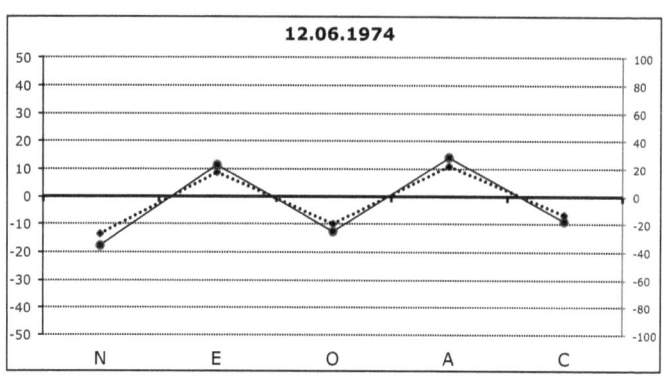

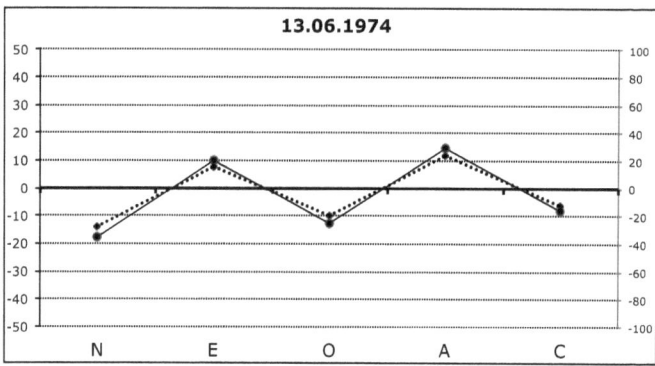

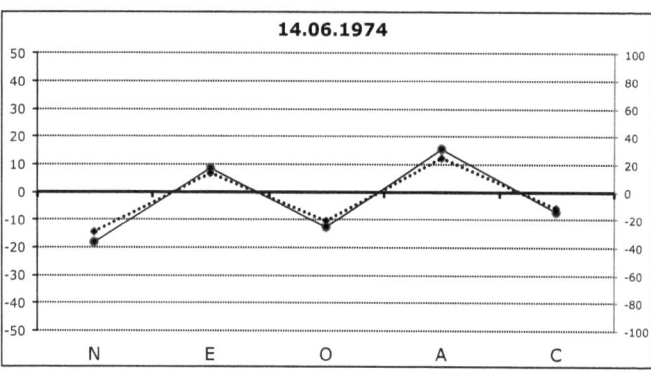

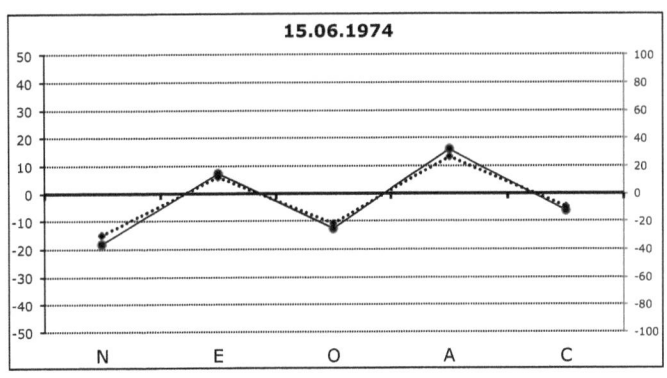

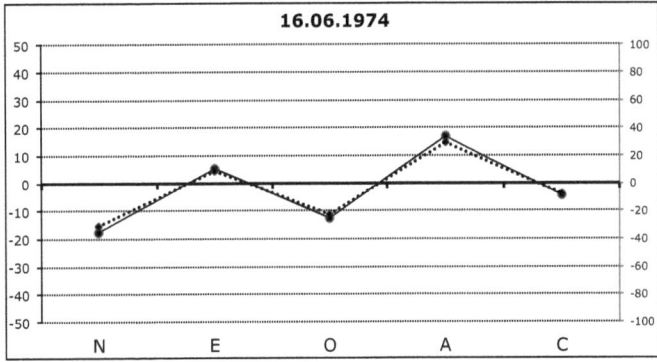

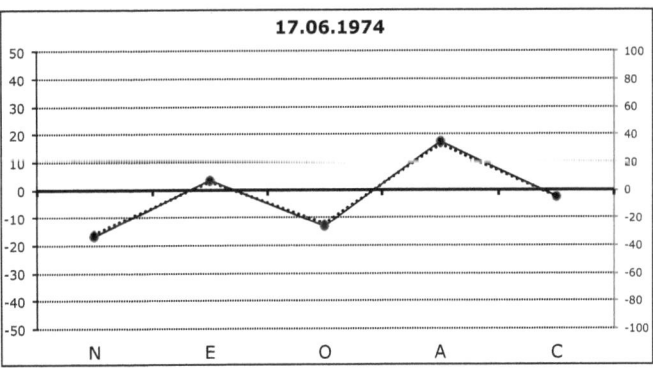

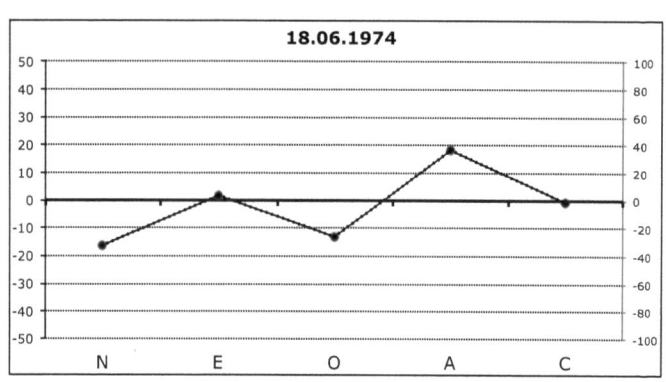

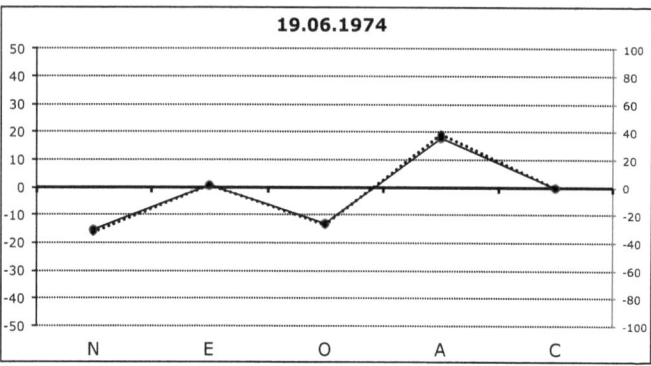

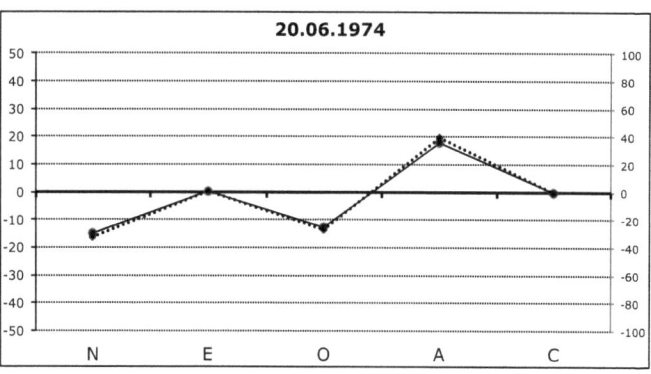

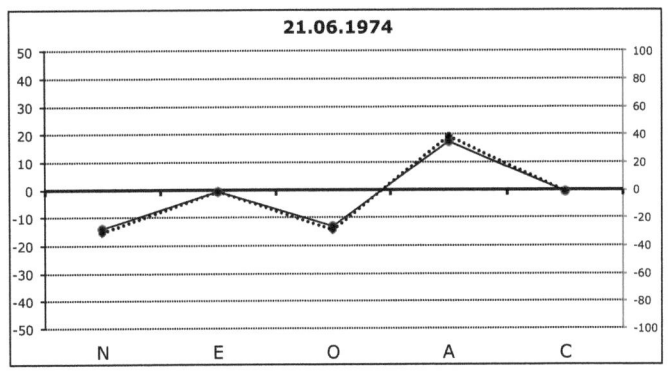

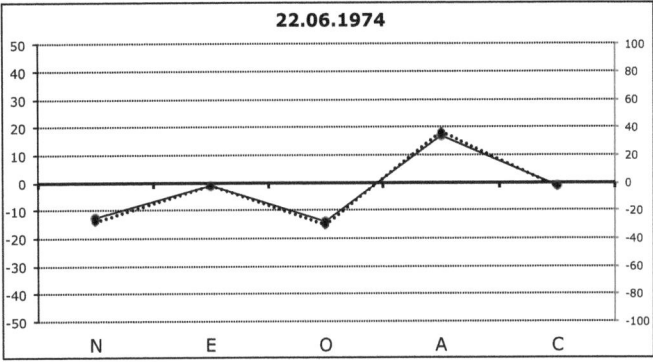

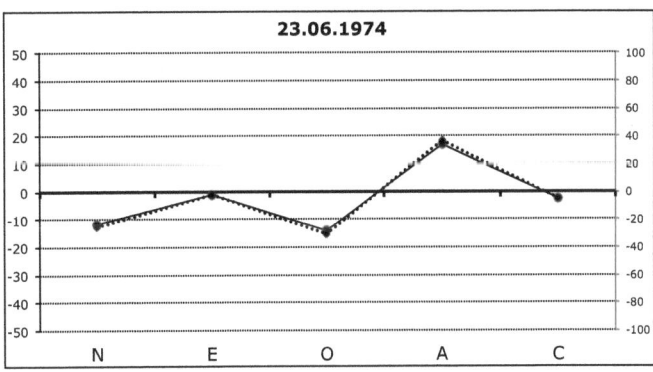

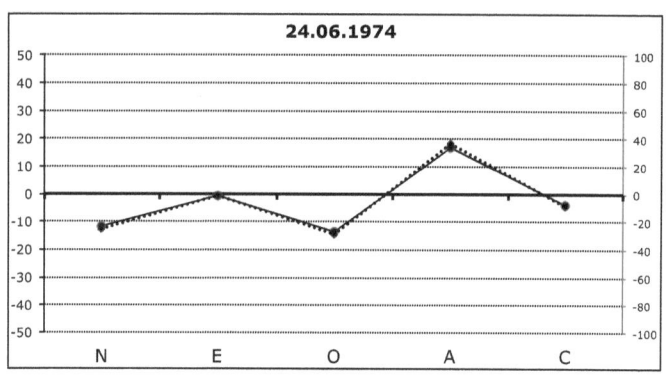

24.06.1974

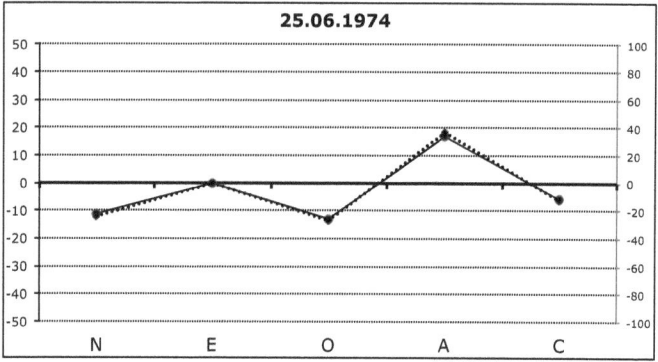

25.06.1974

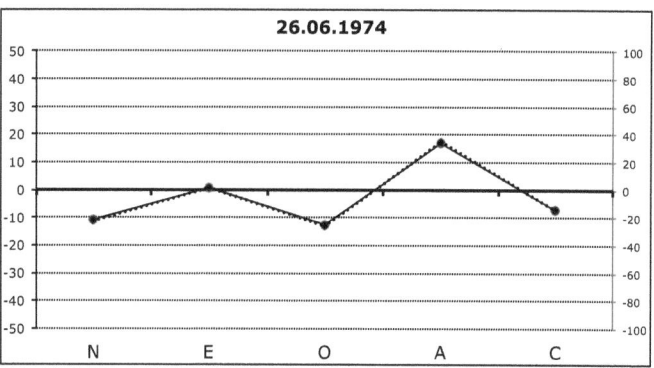

26.06.1974

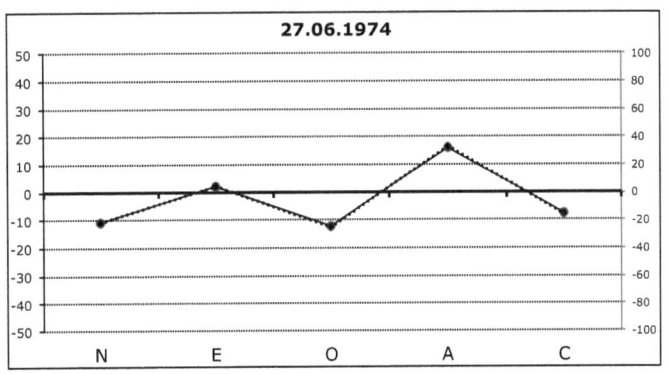

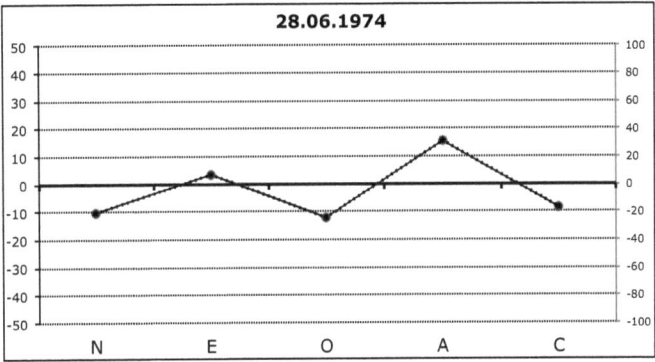

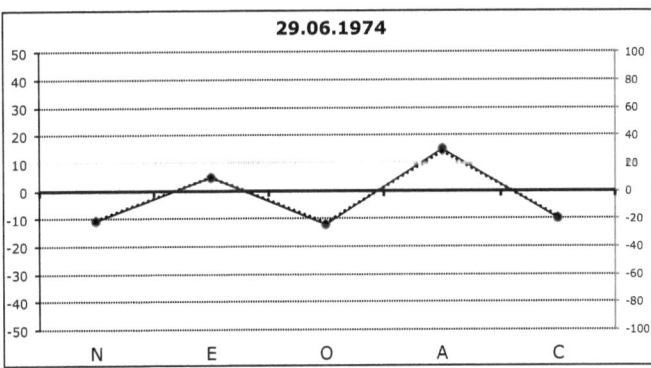

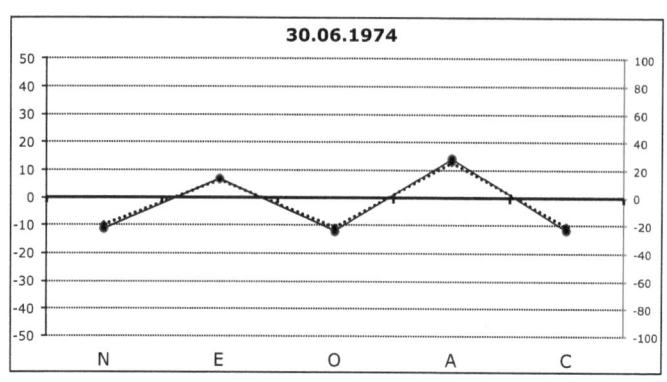

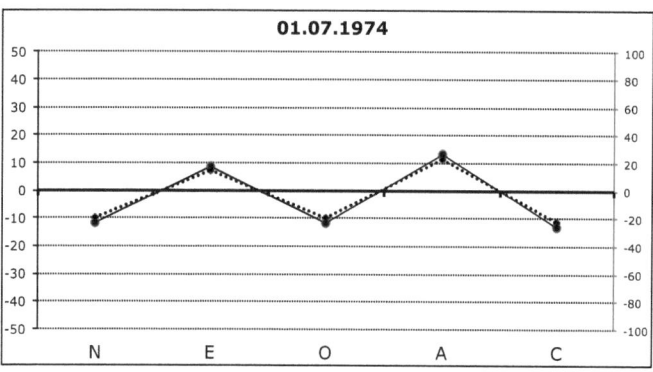

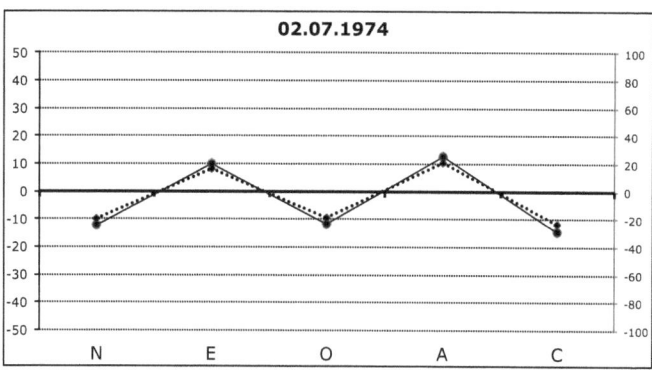

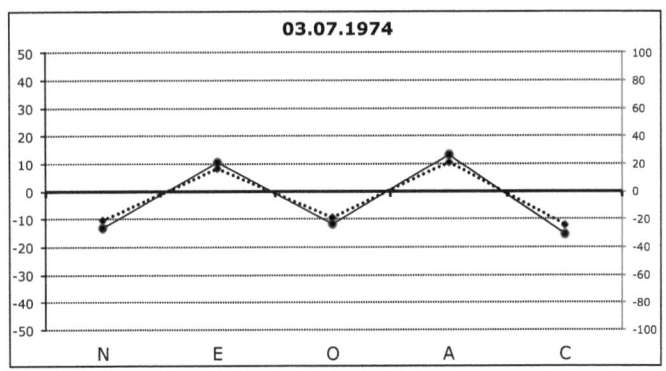

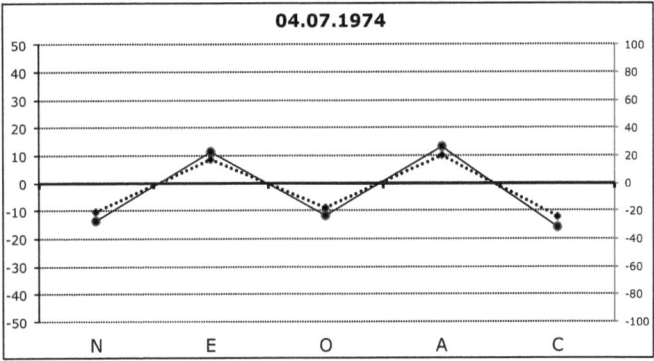

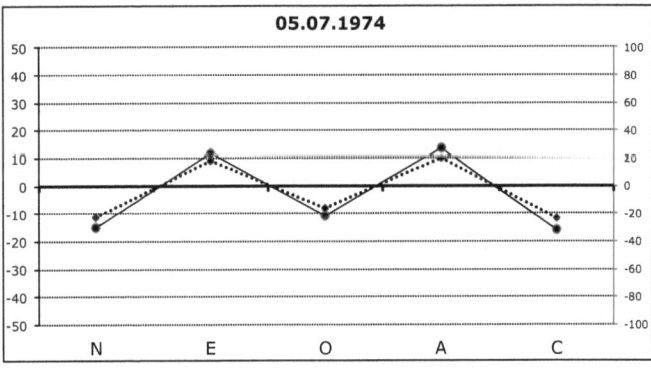

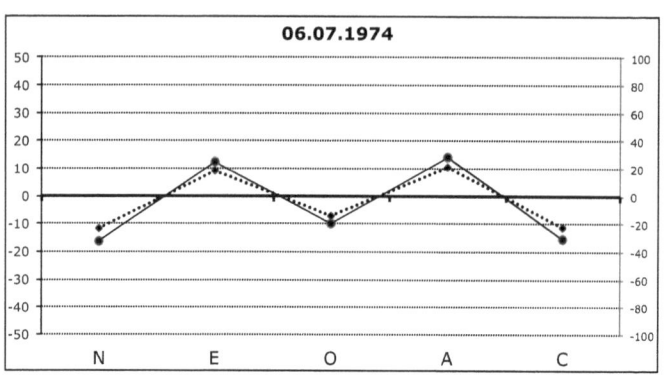

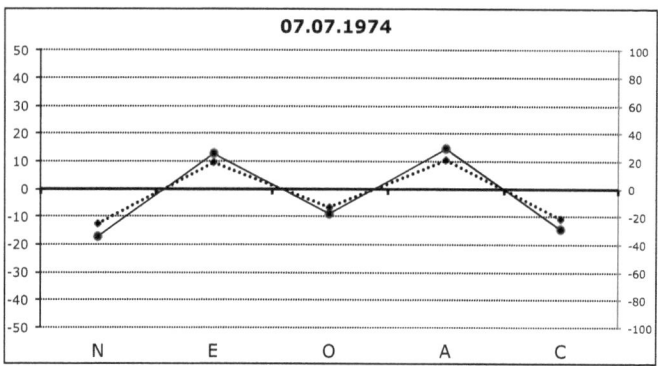

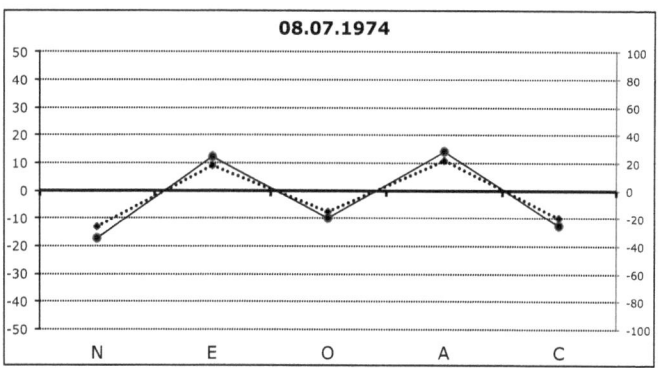

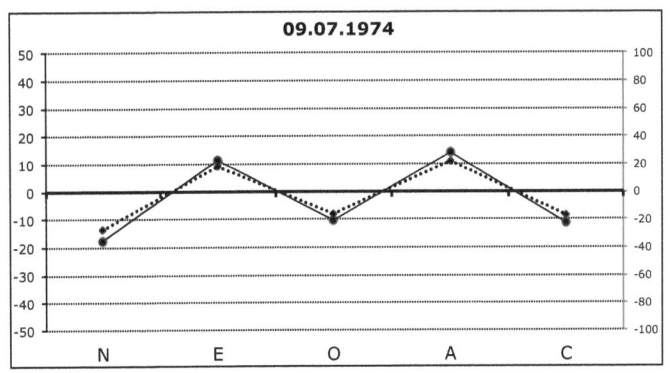

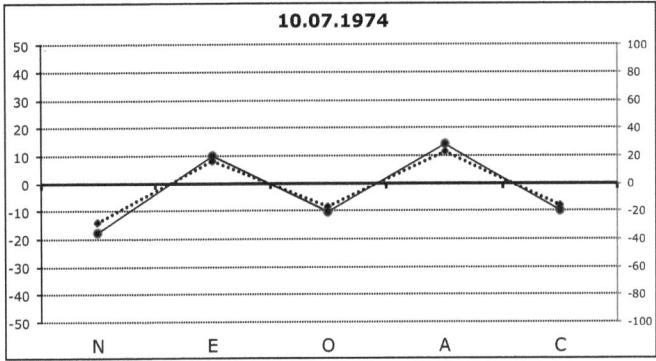

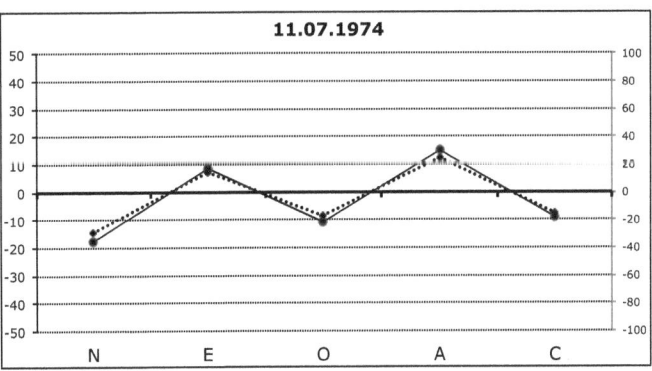

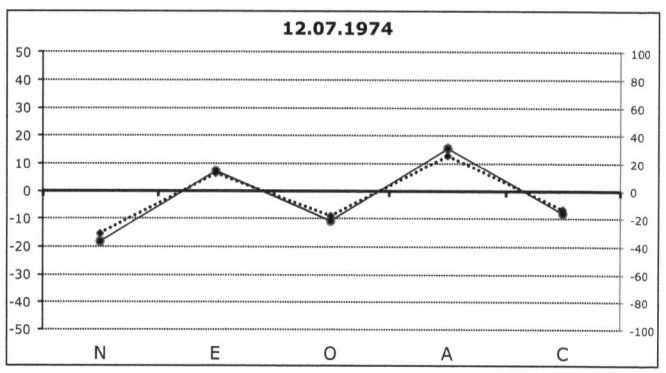

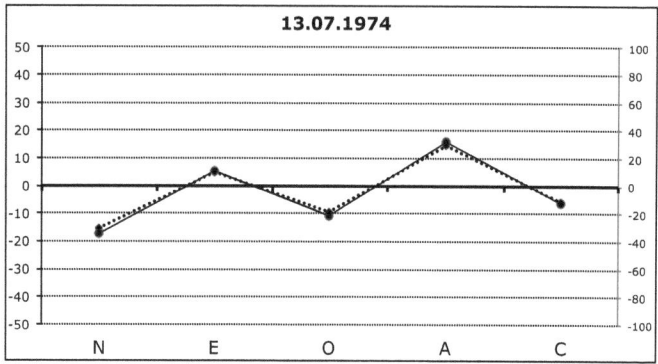

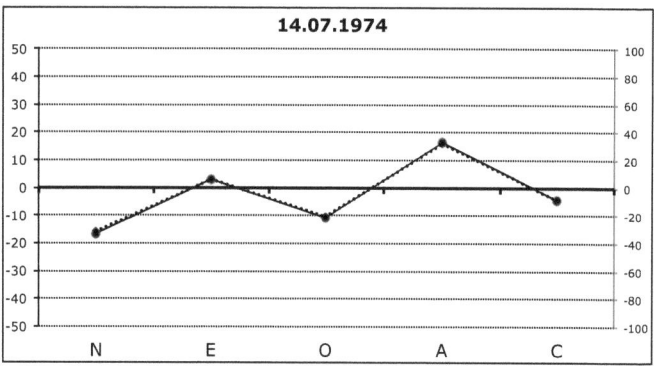

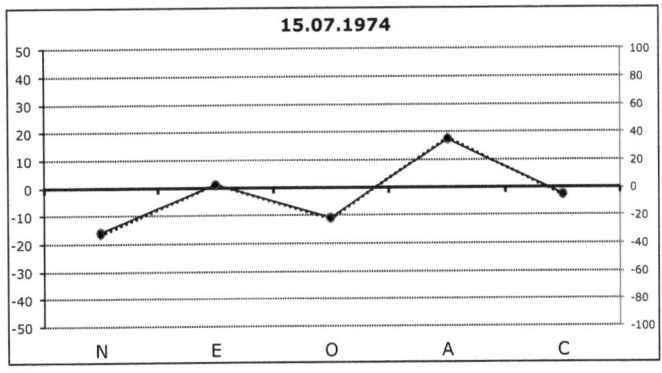

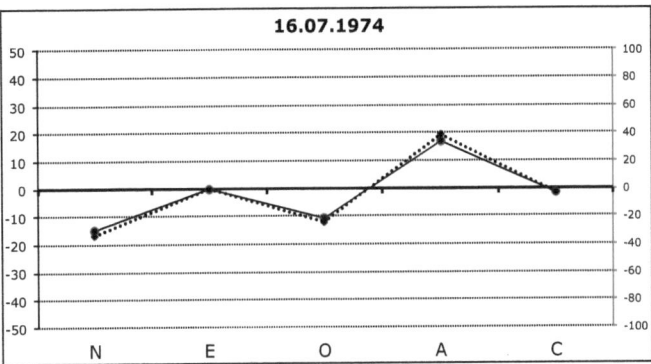

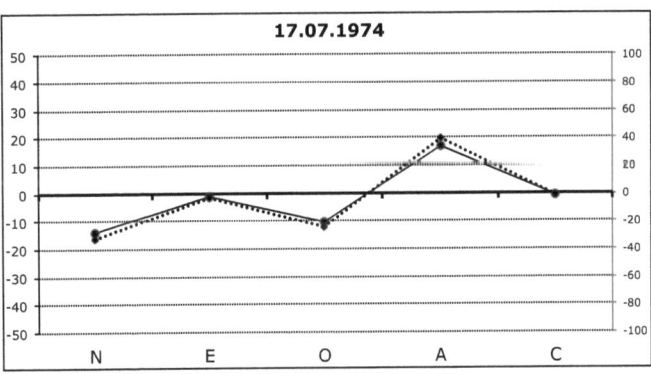

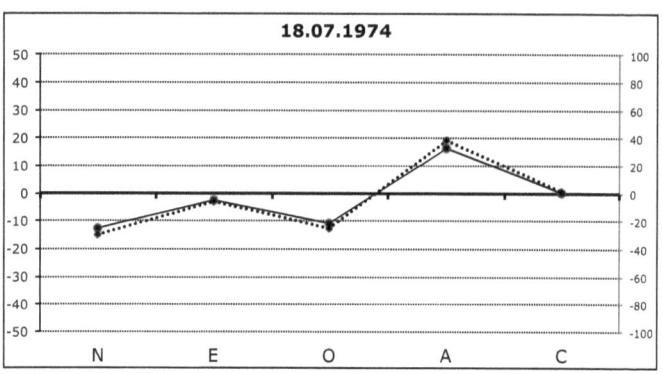

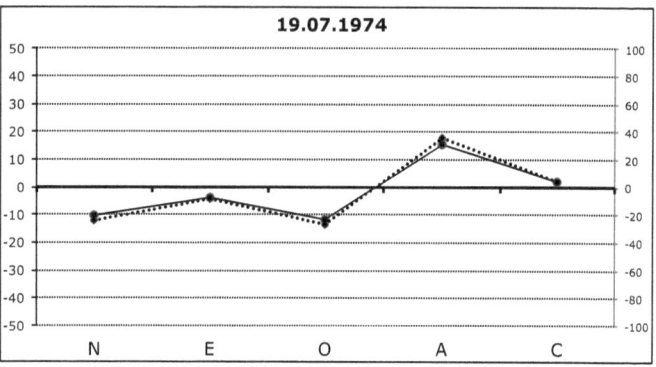

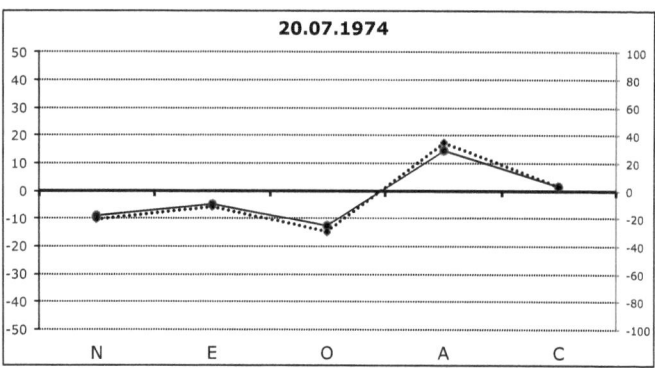

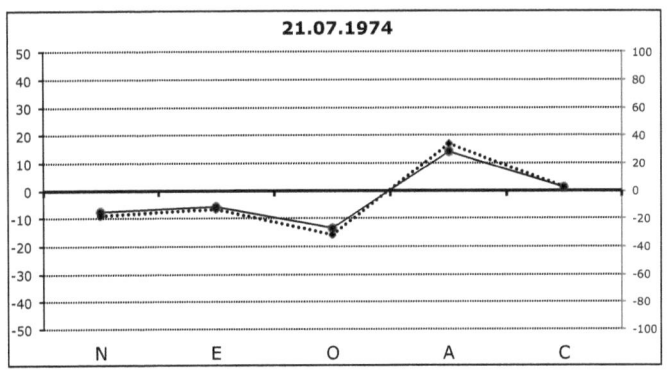

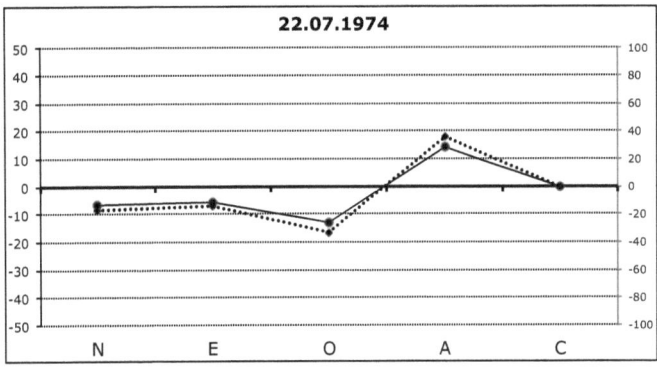

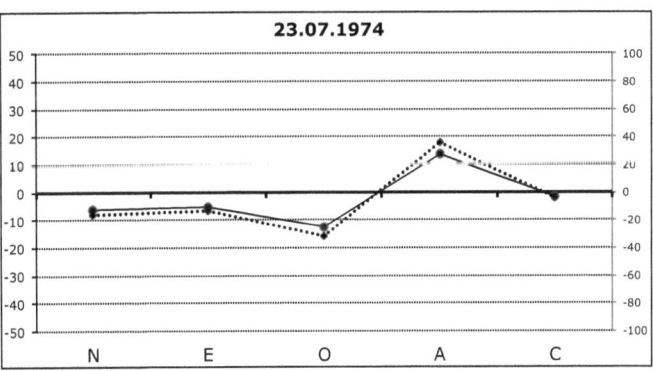

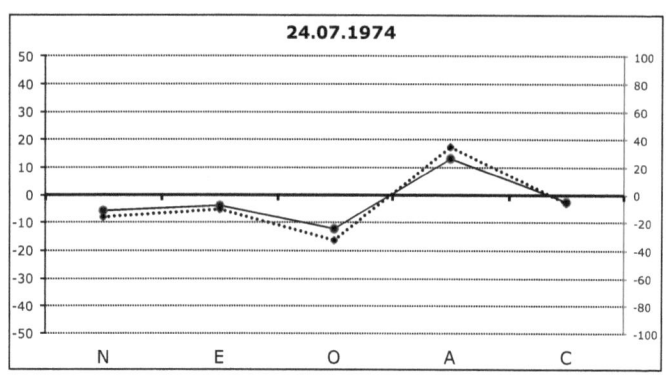

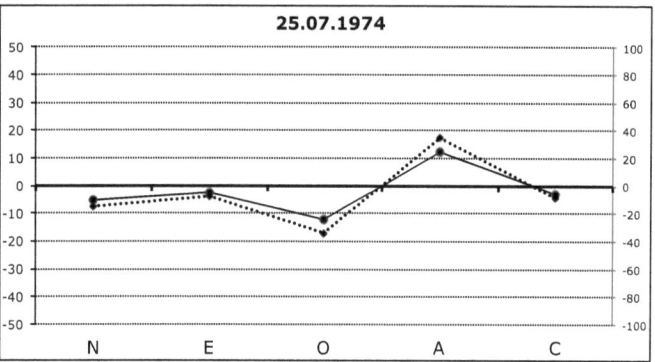

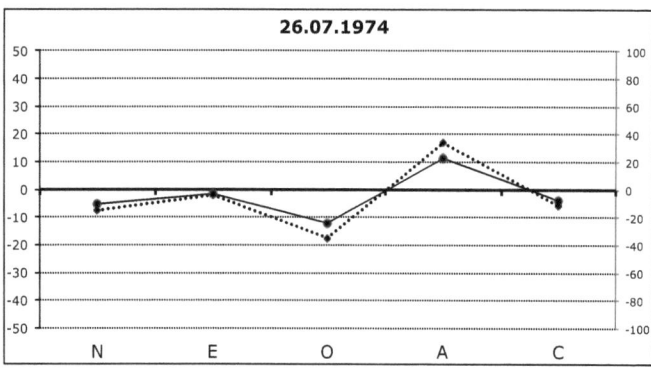

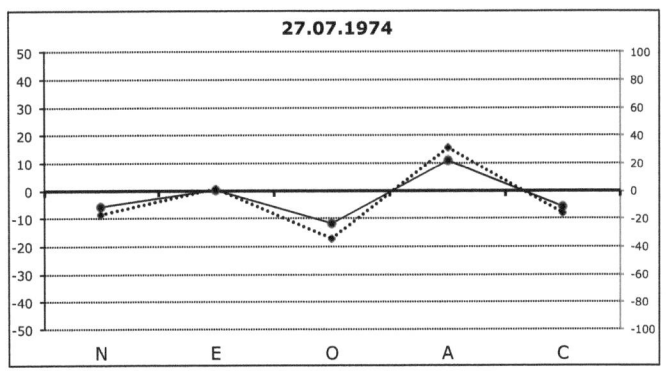

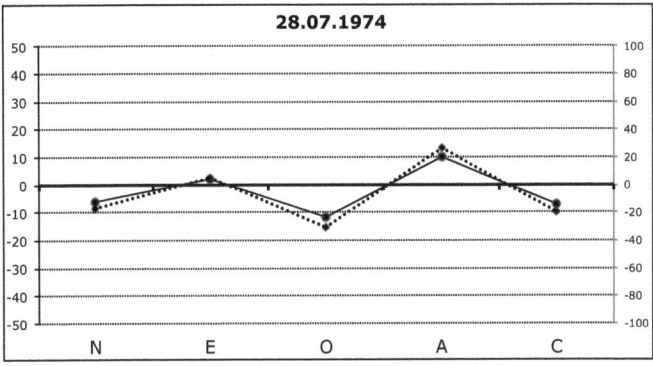

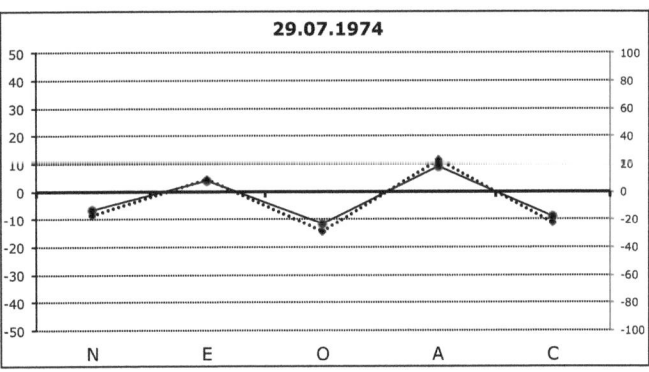

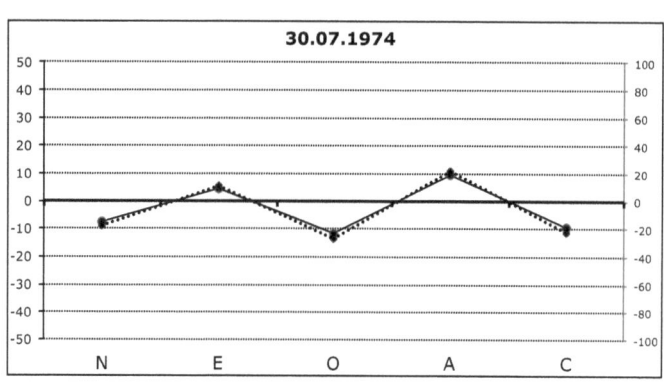

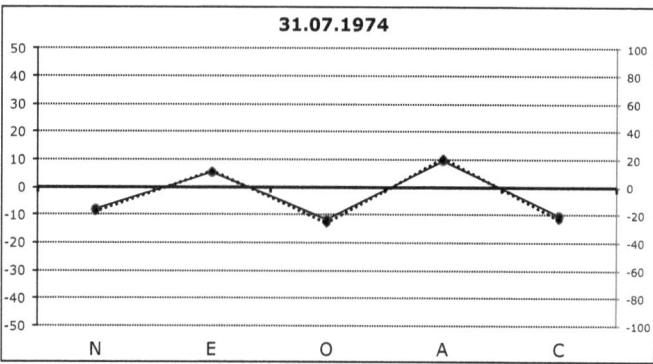

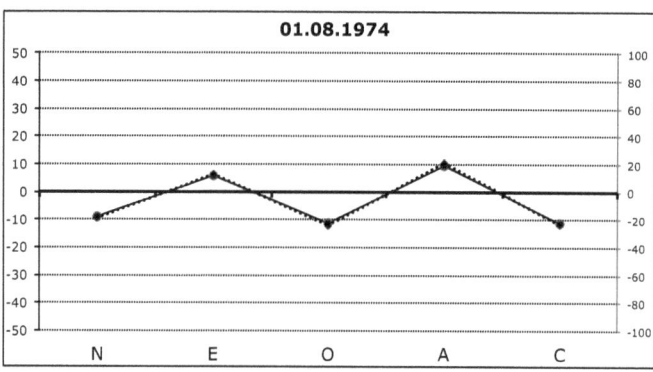

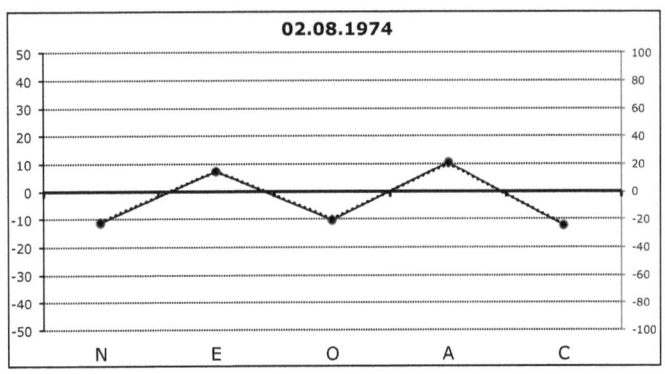

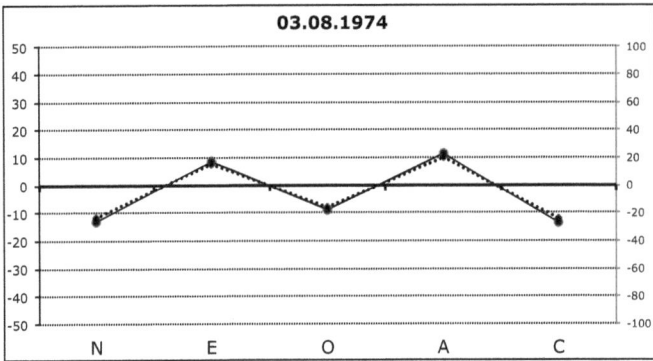

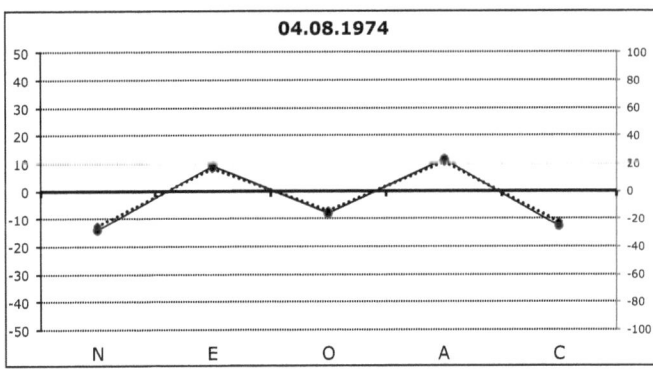

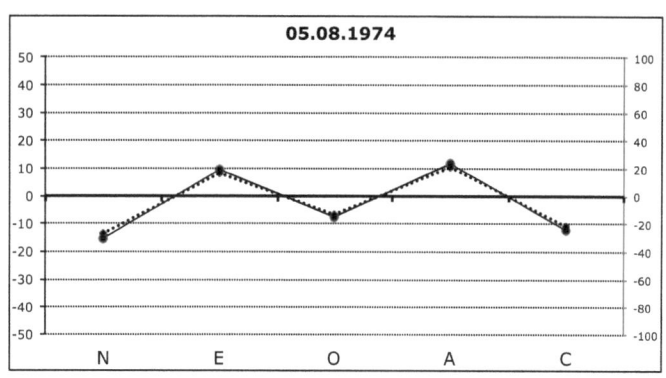

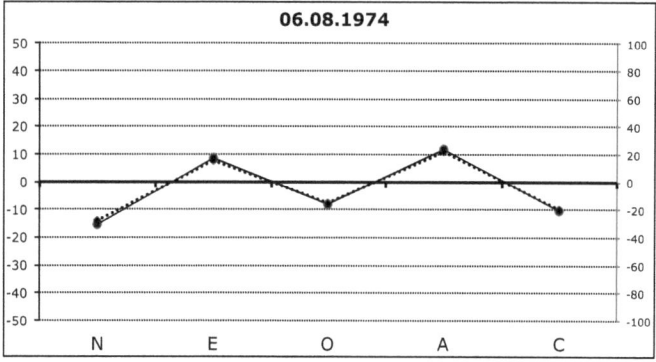

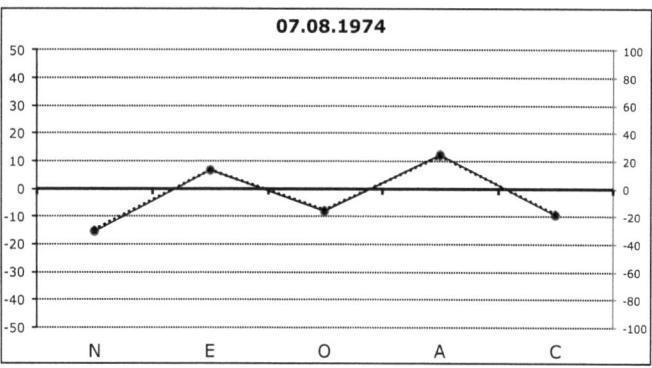

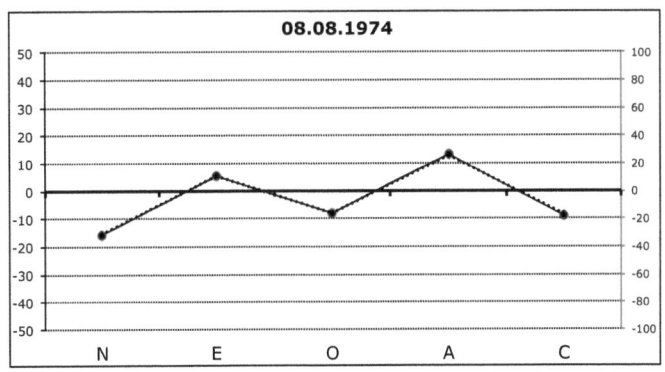

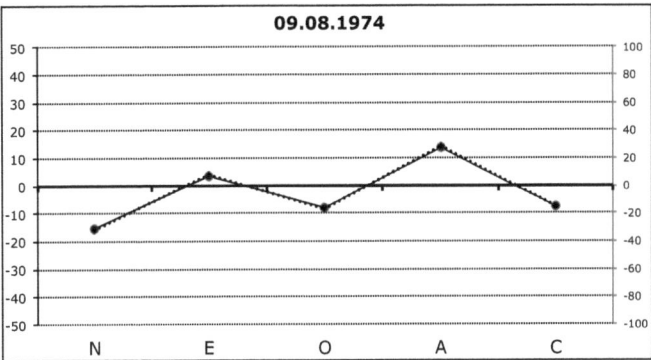

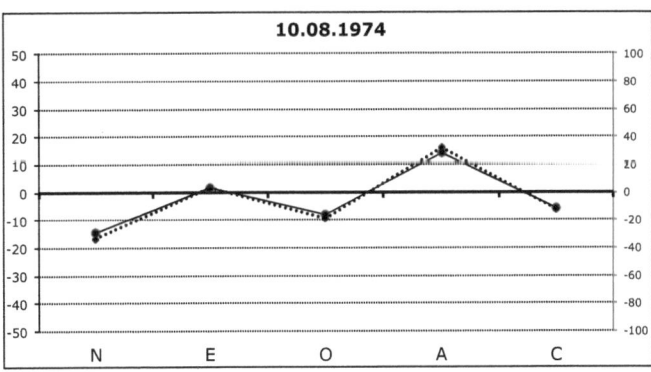

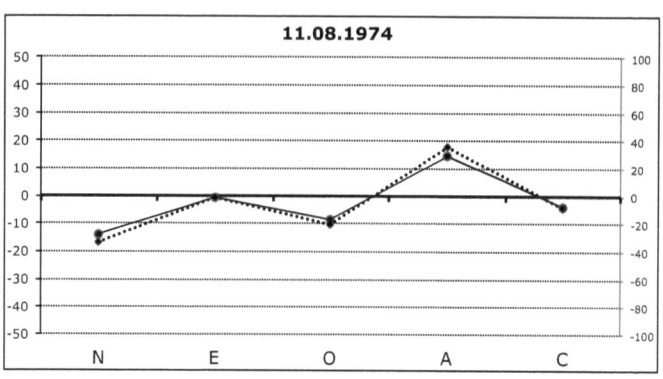

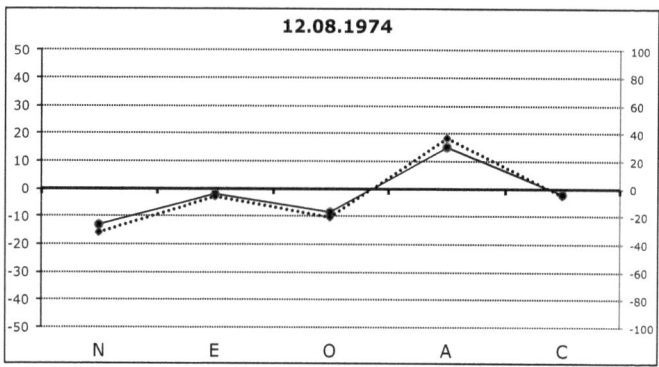

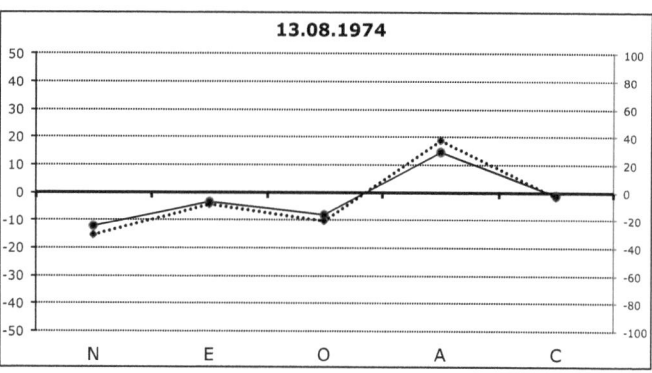

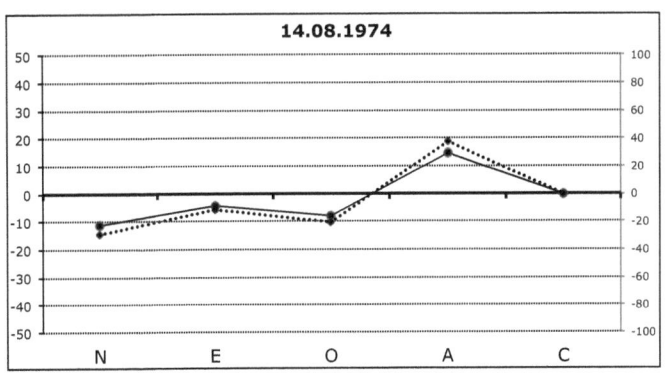

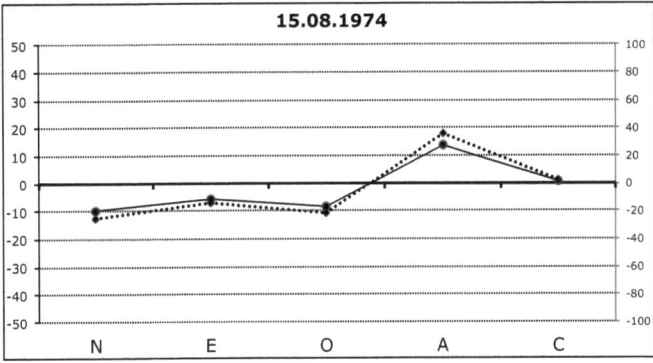

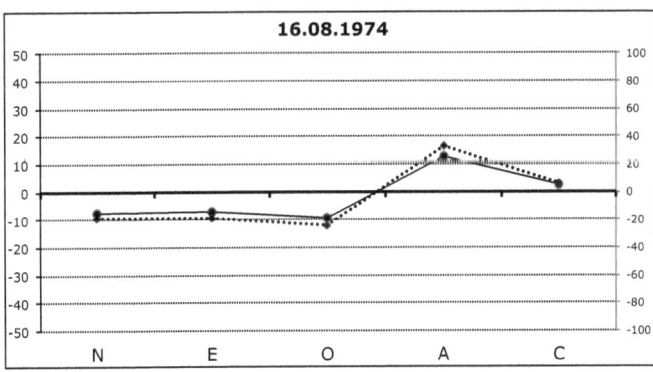

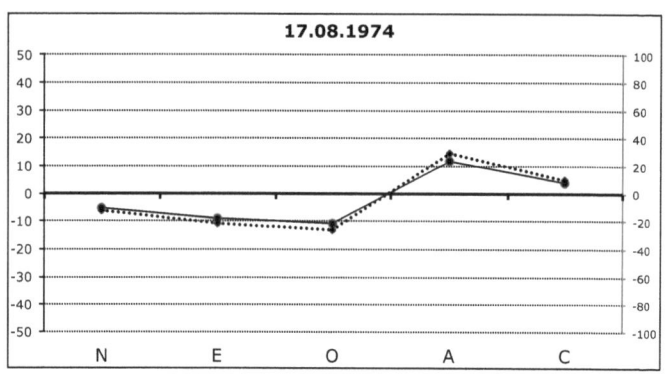

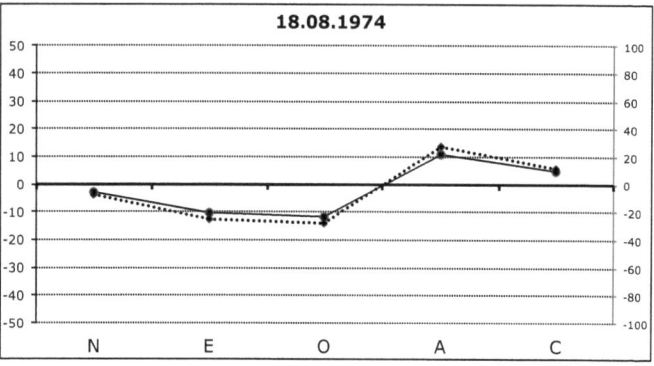

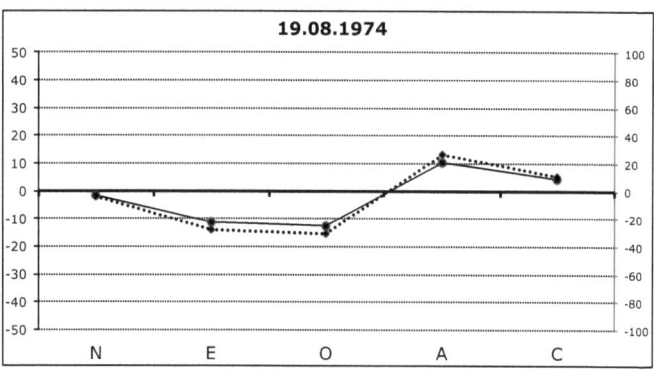

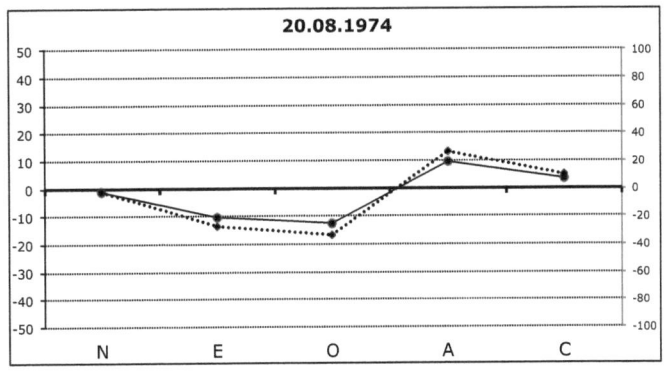

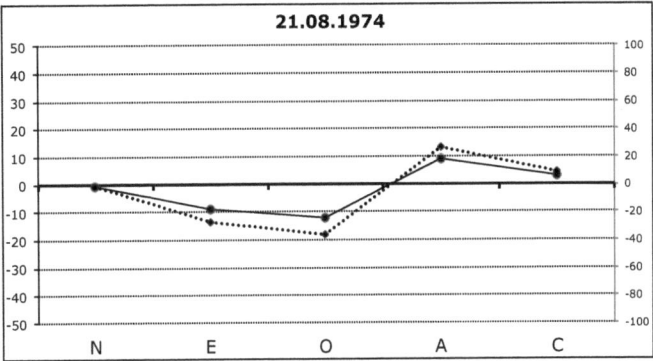

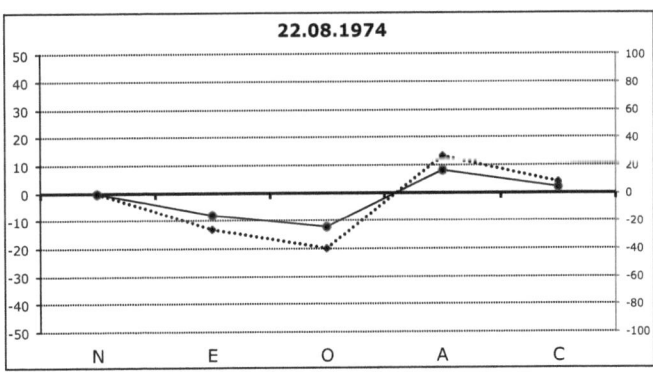

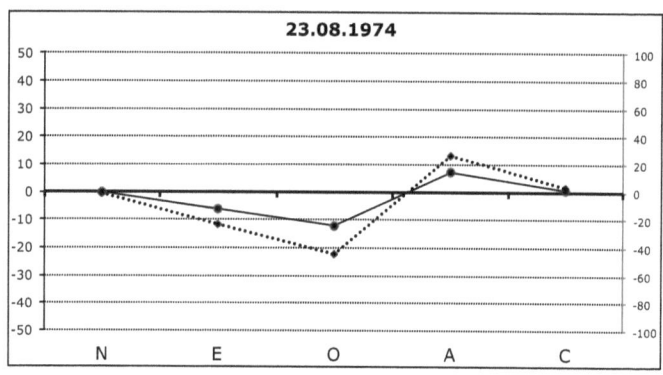

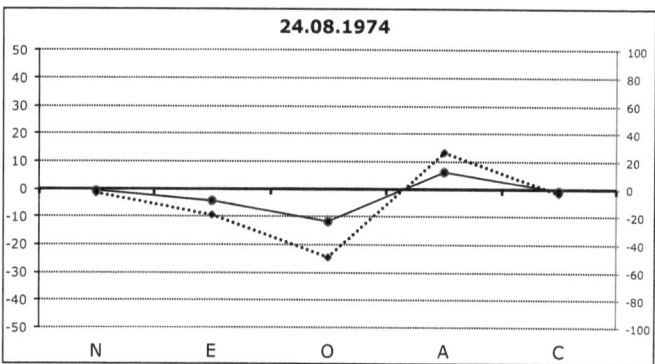

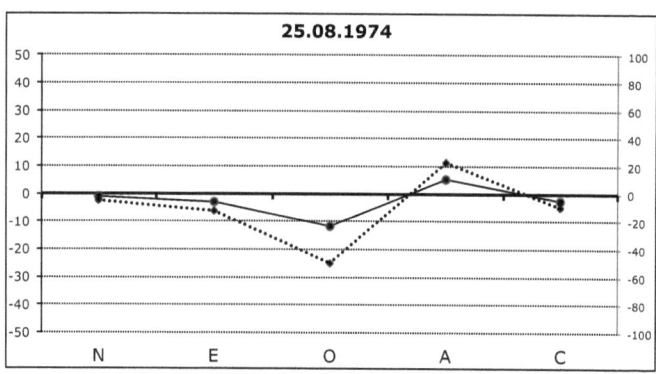

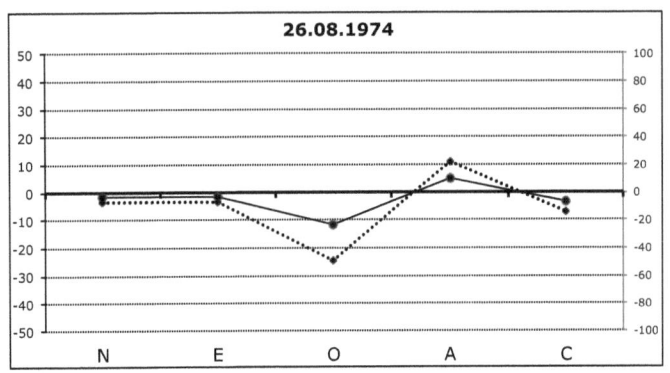

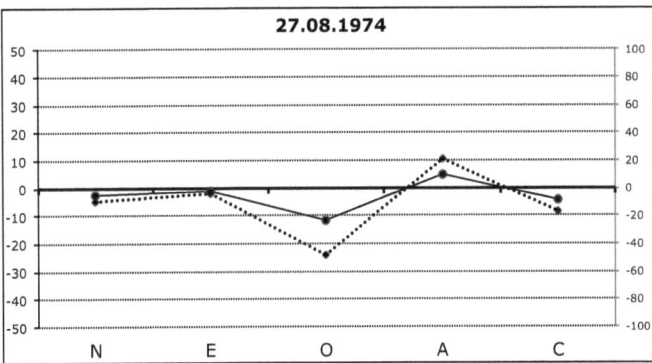

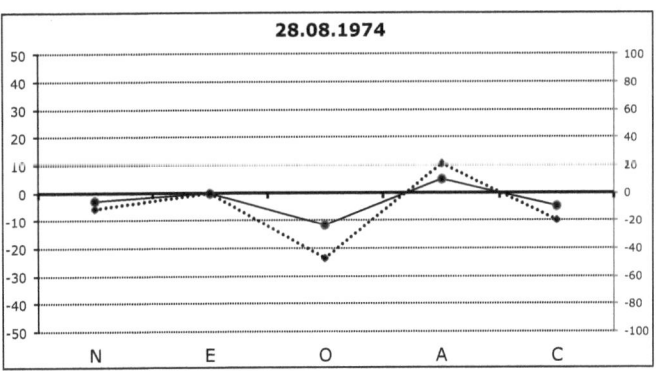

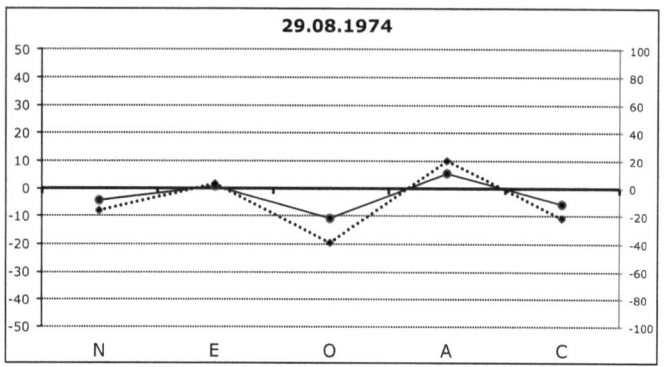

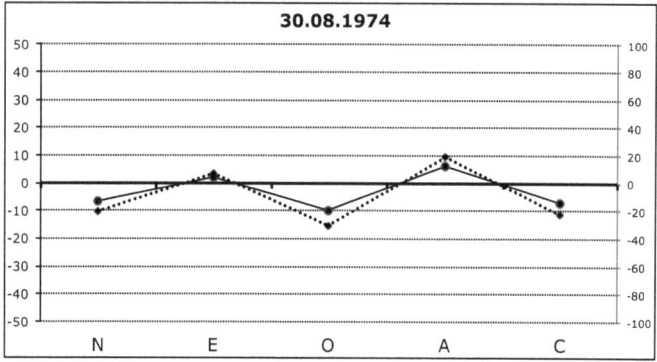

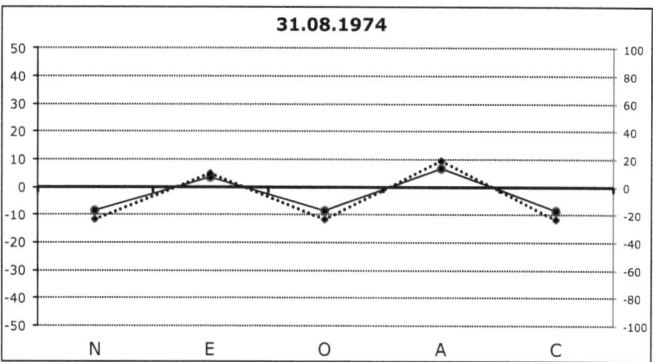

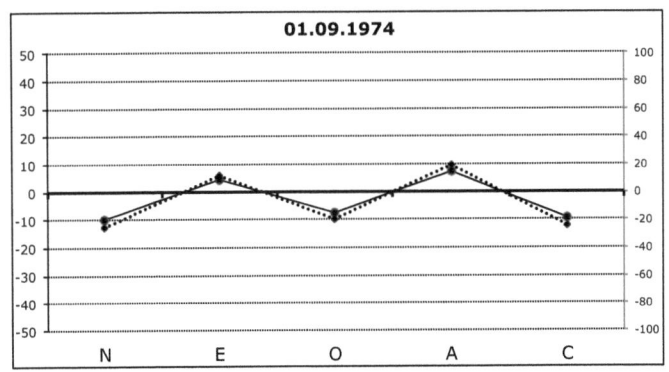

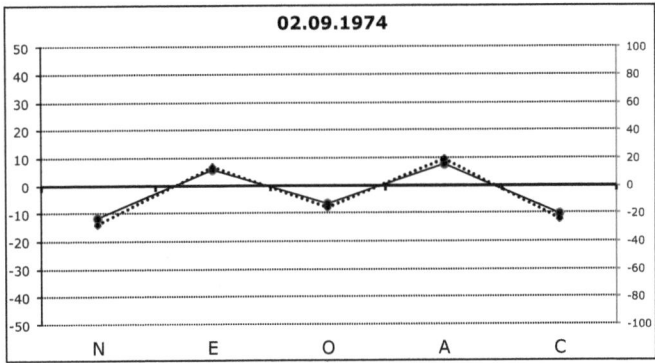

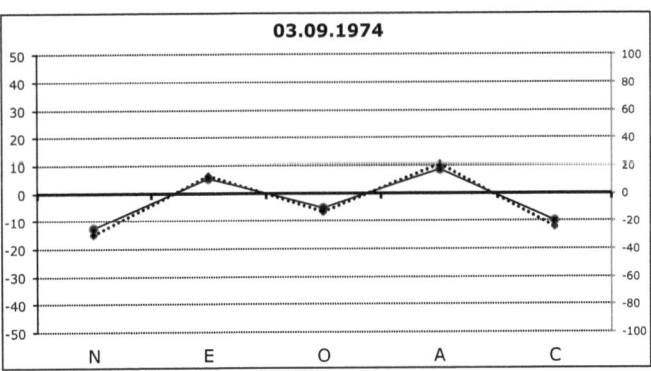

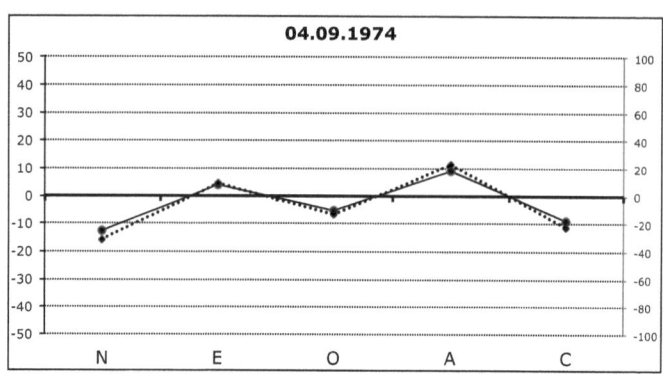

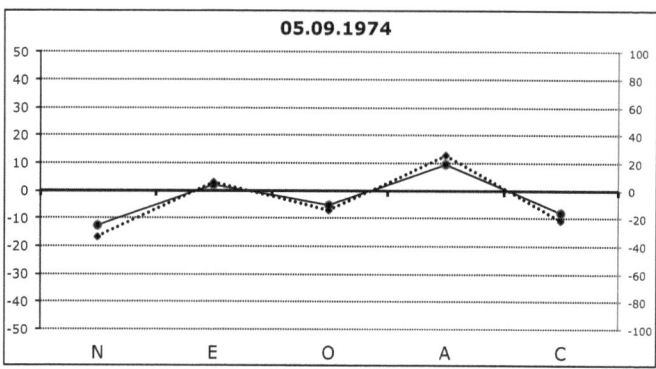

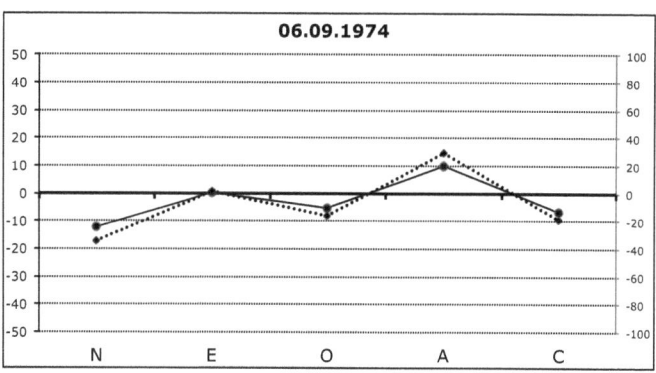

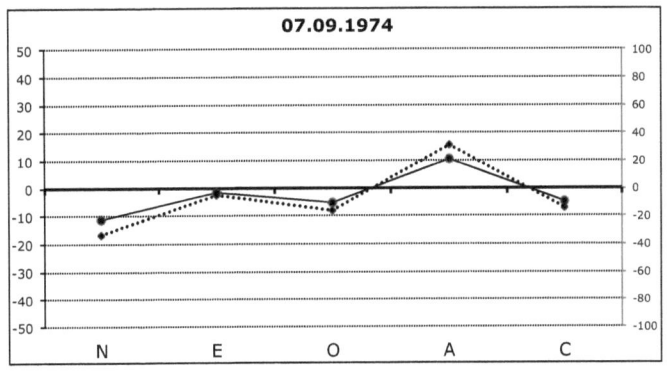

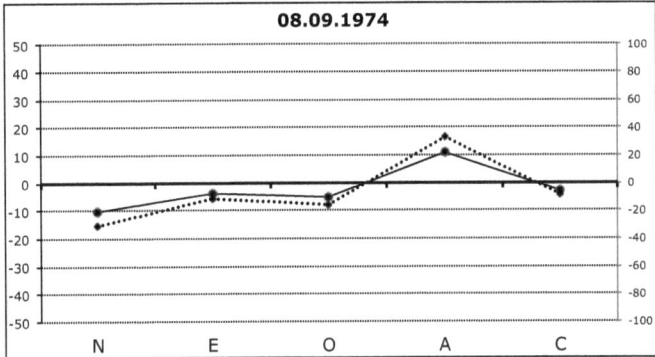

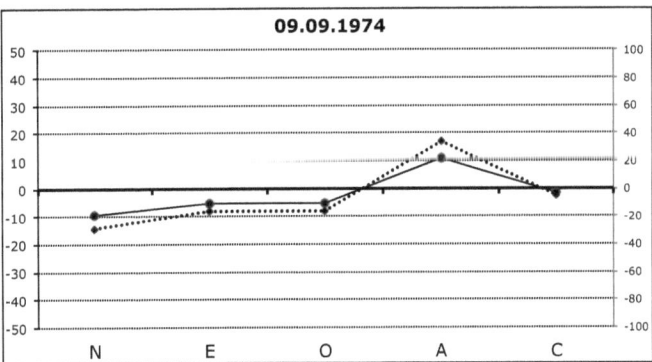

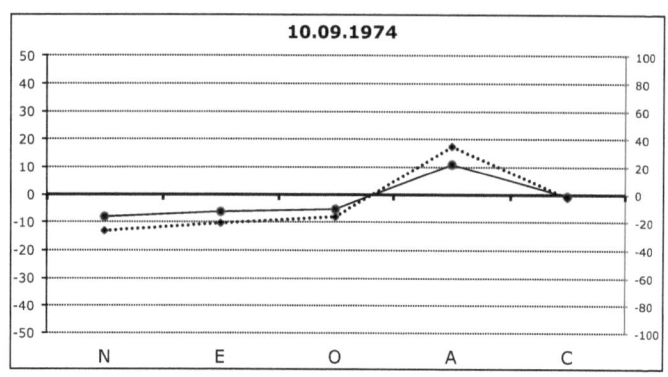

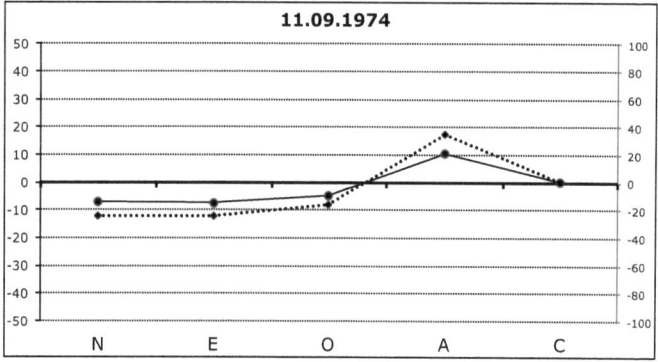

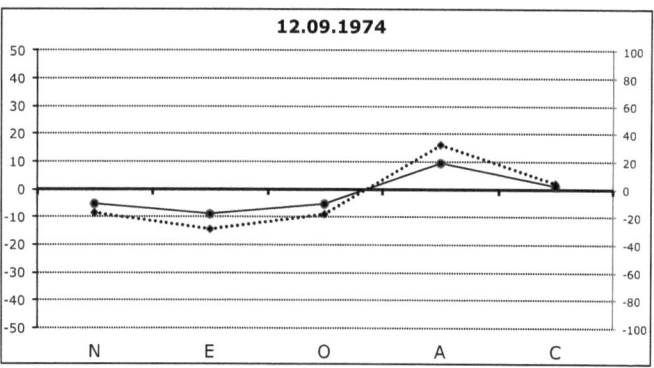

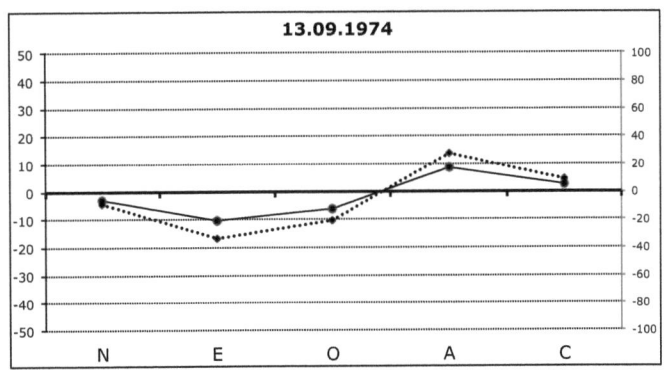

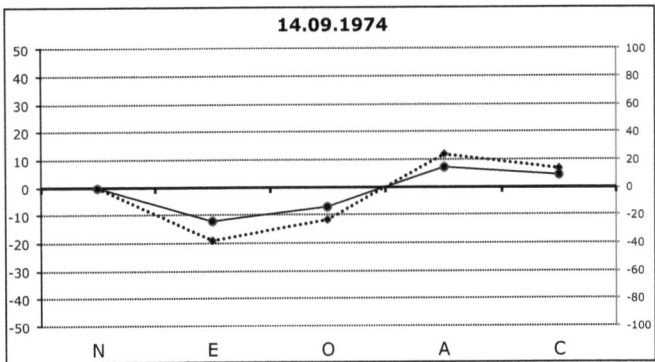

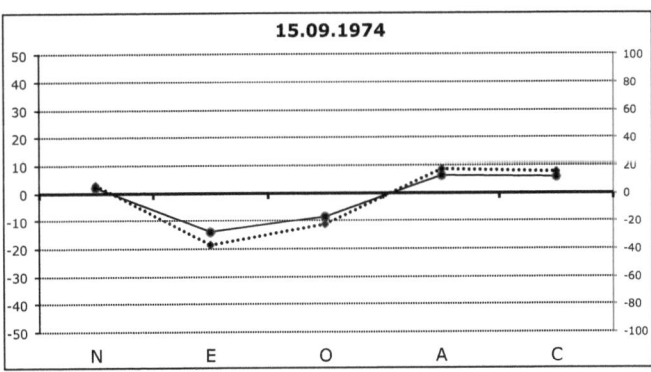

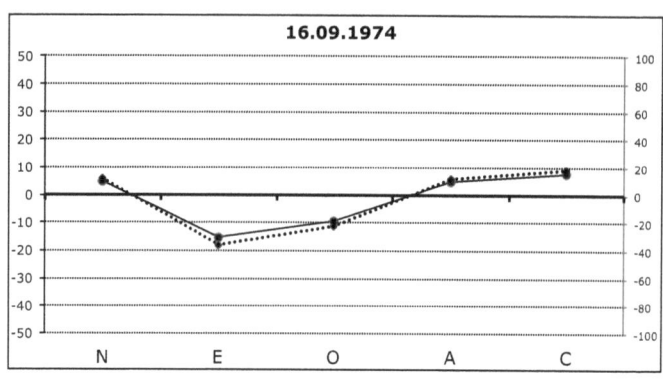

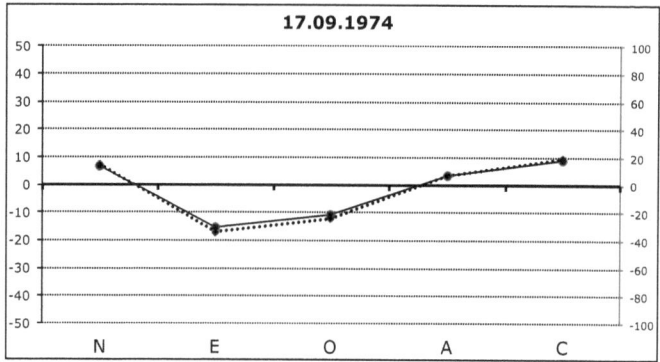

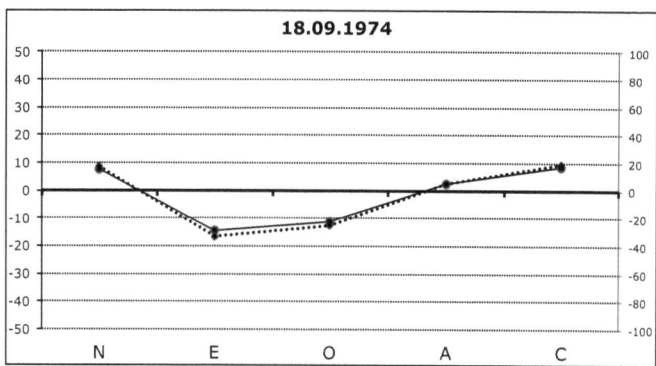

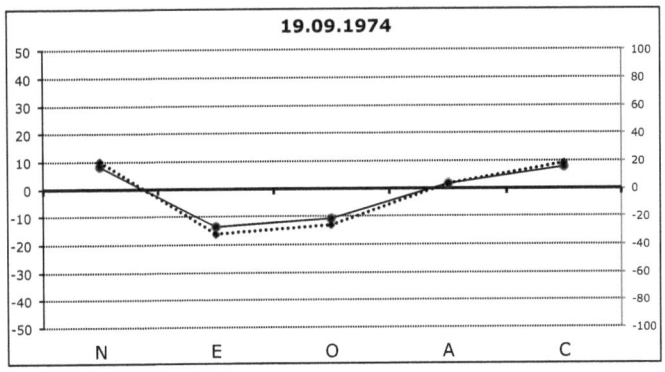

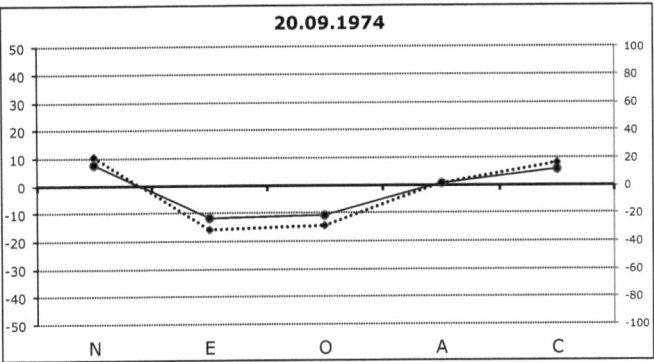

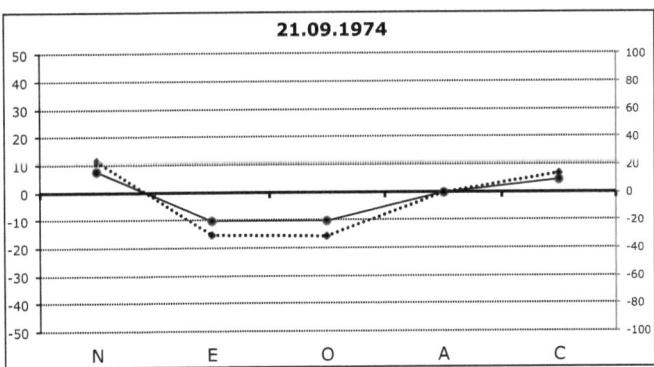

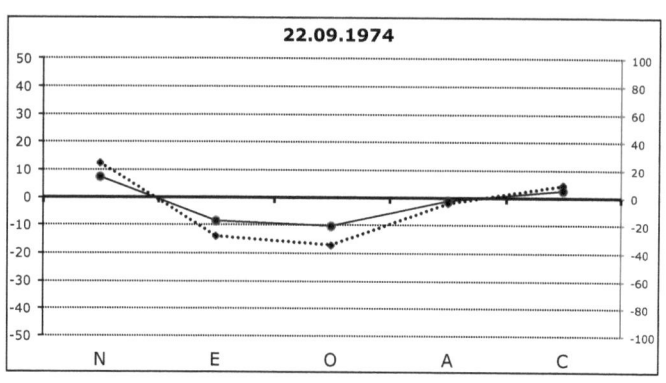

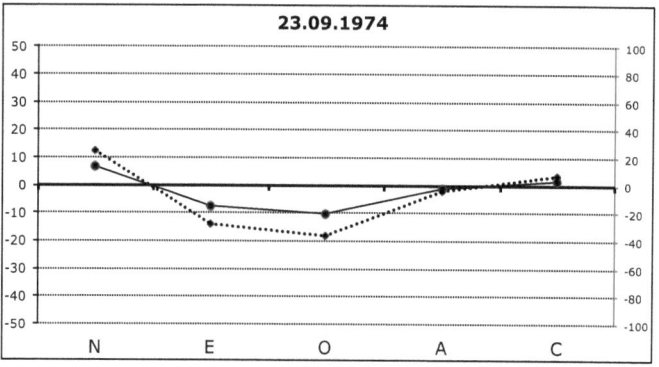

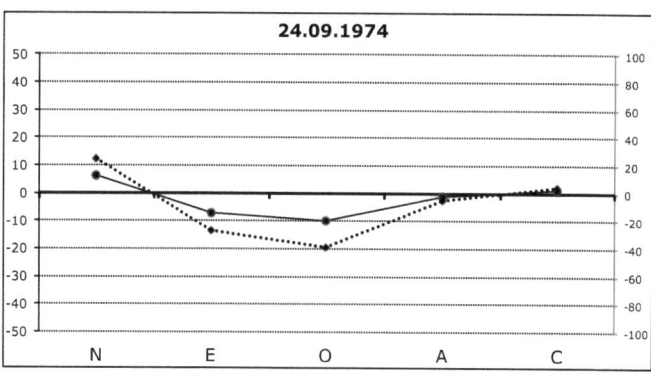

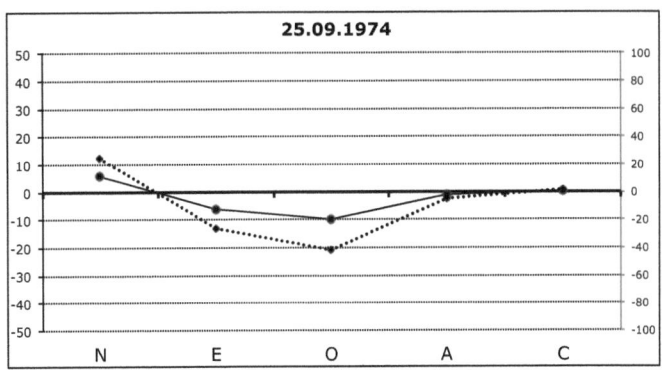

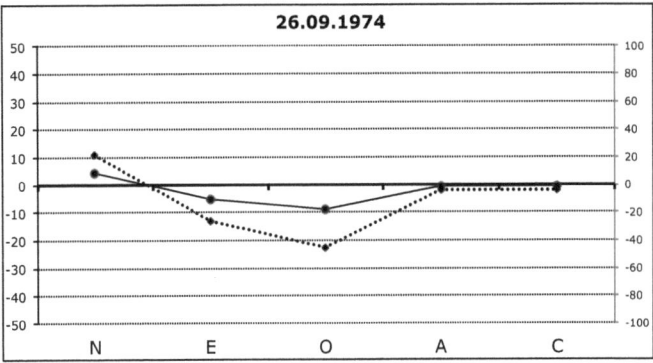

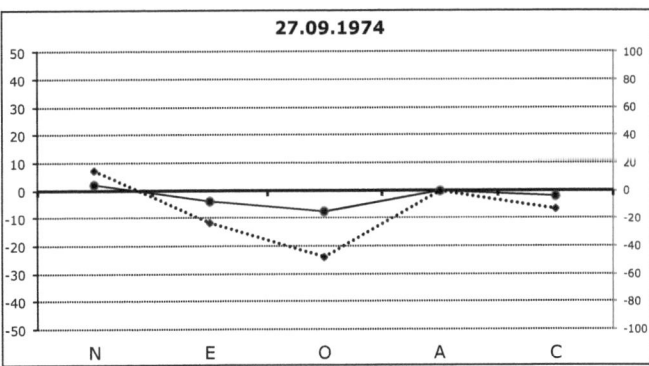

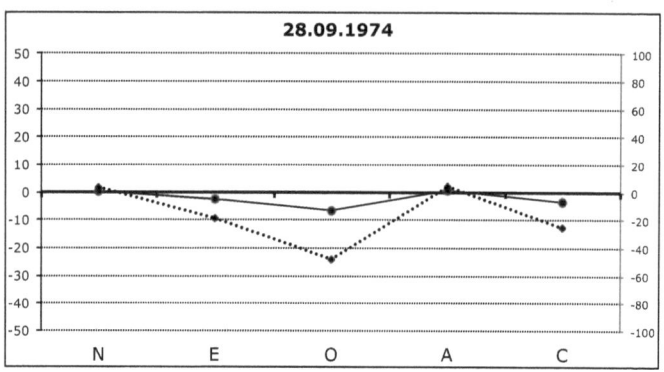

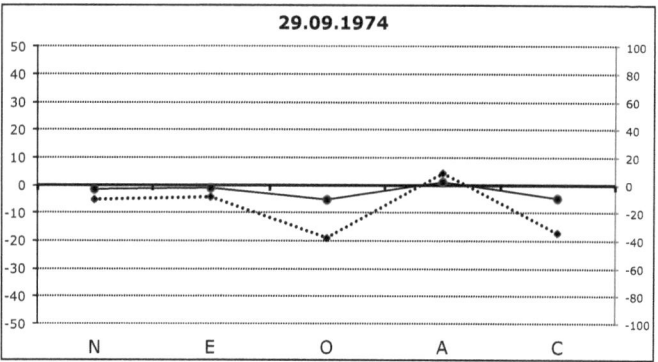

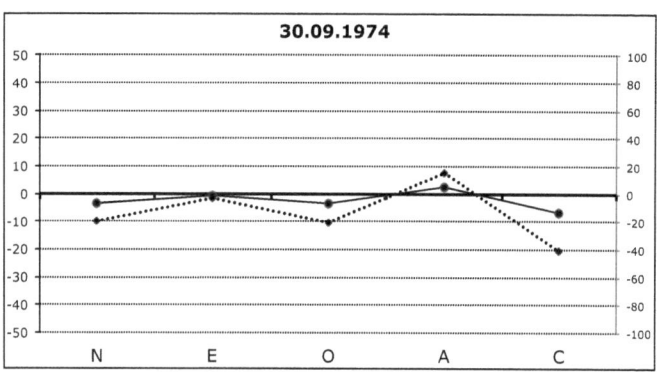

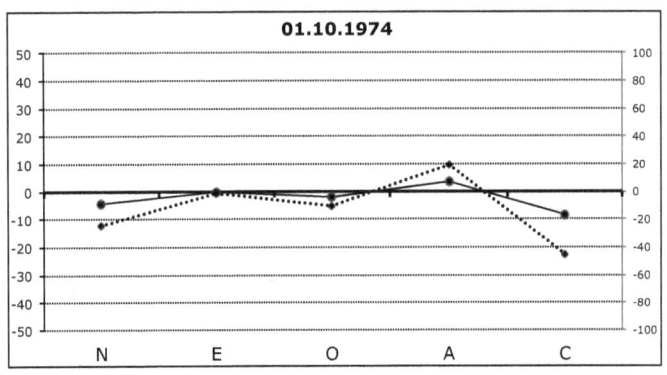

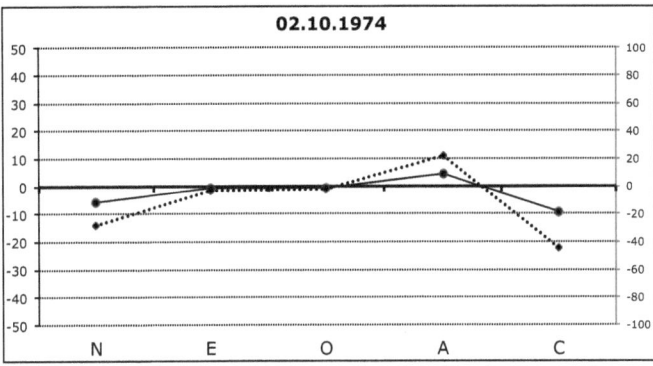

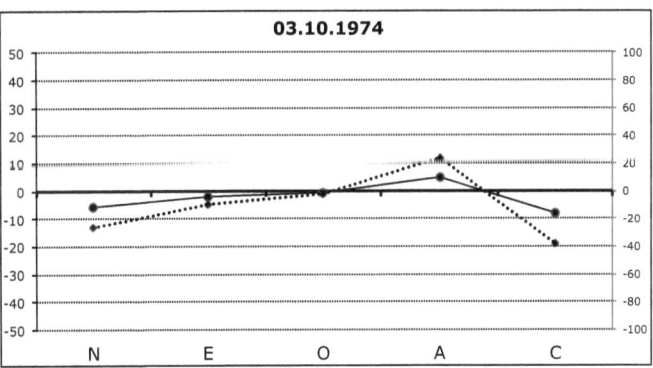

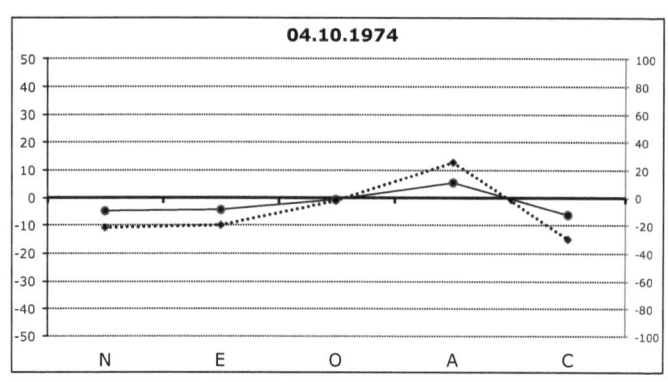

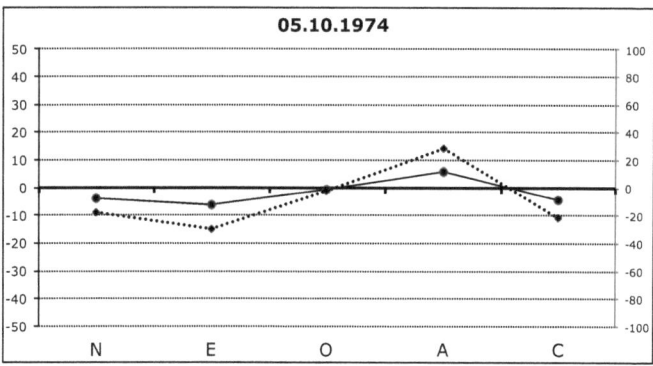

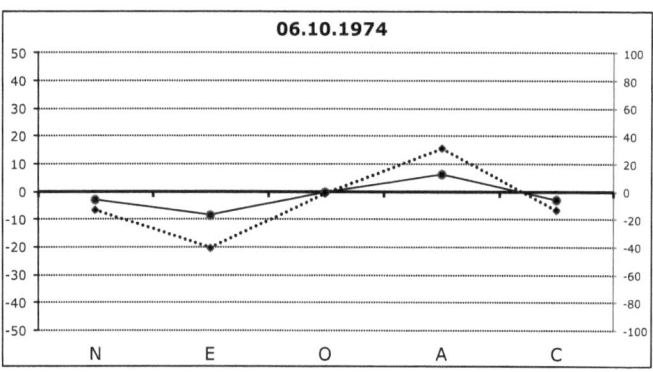

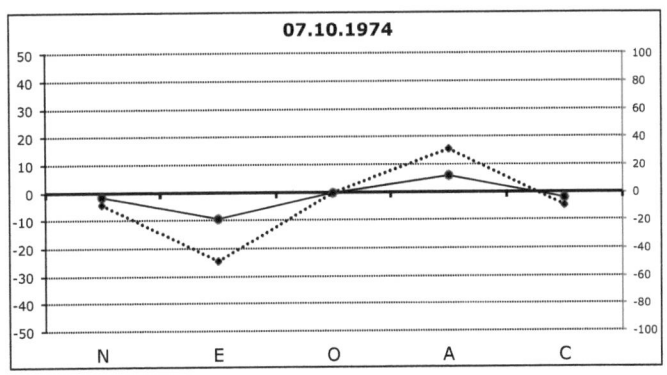

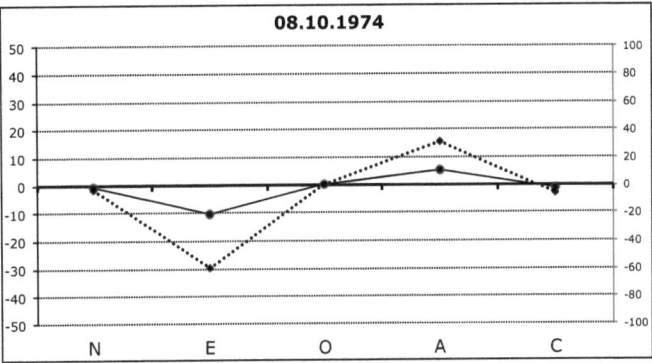

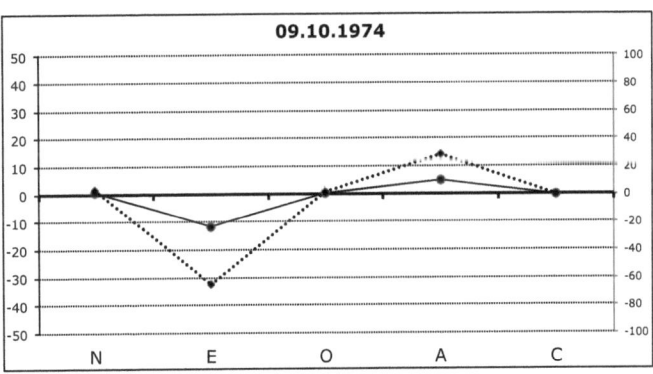

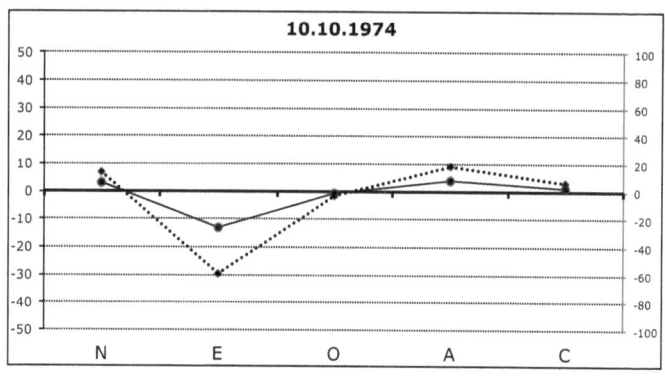

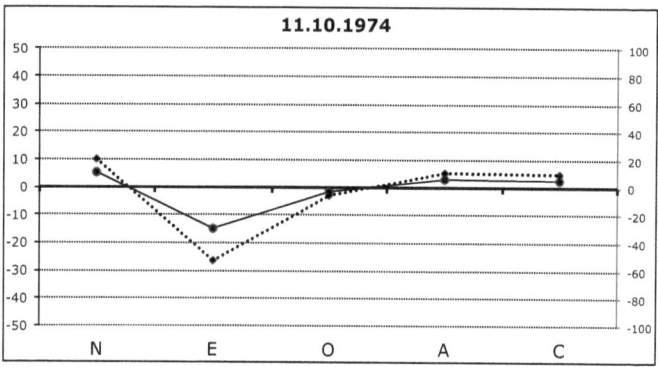

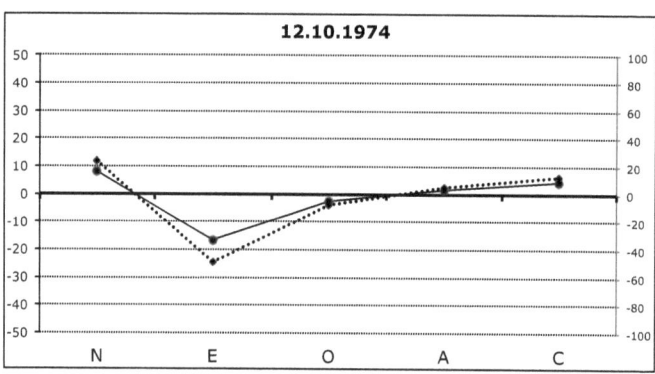

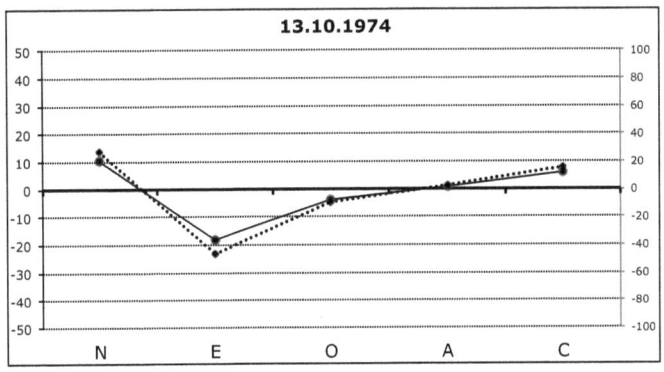

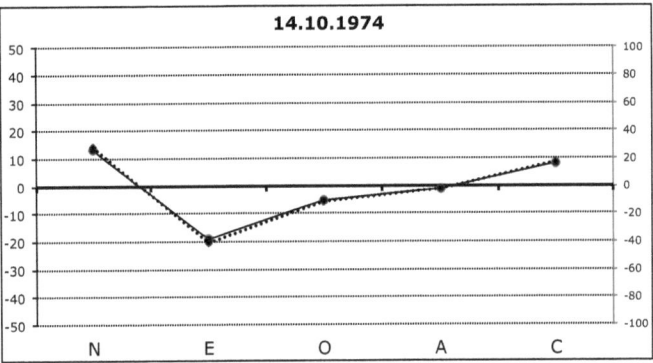

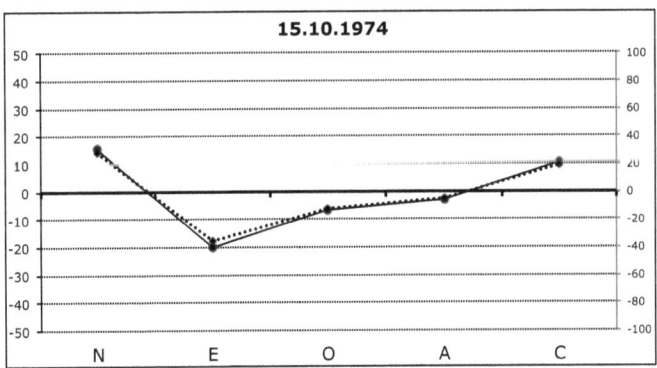

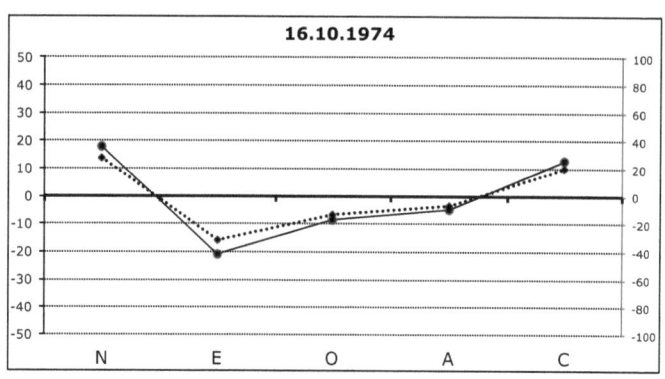

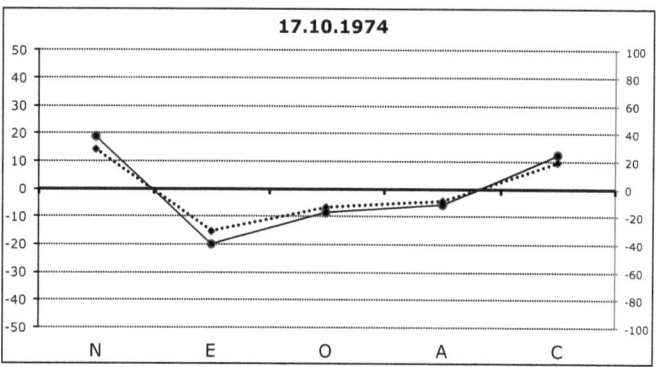

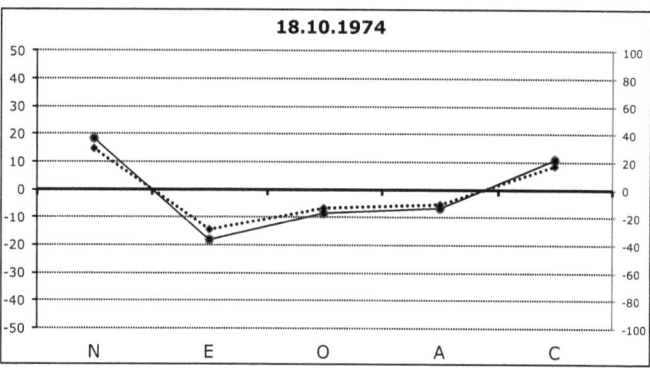

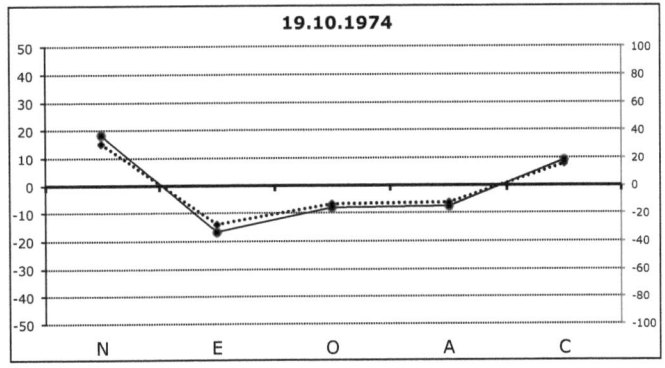

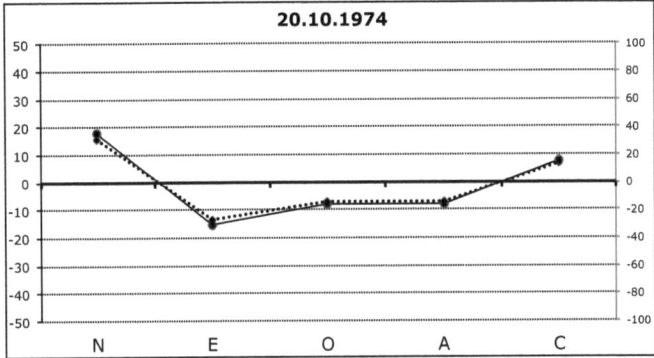

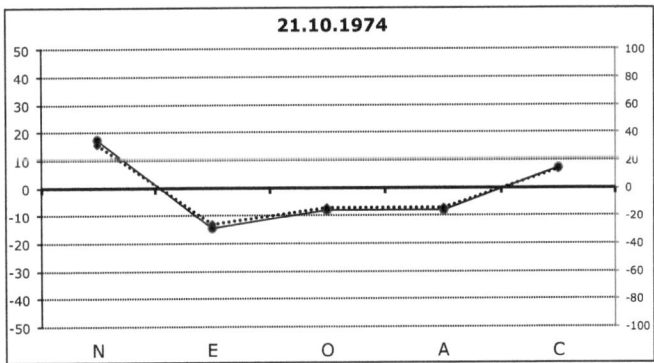

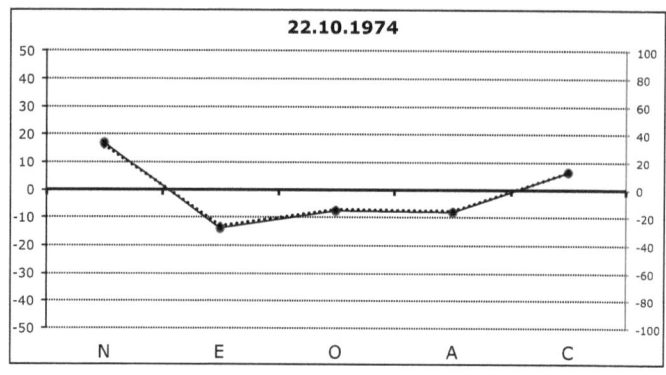

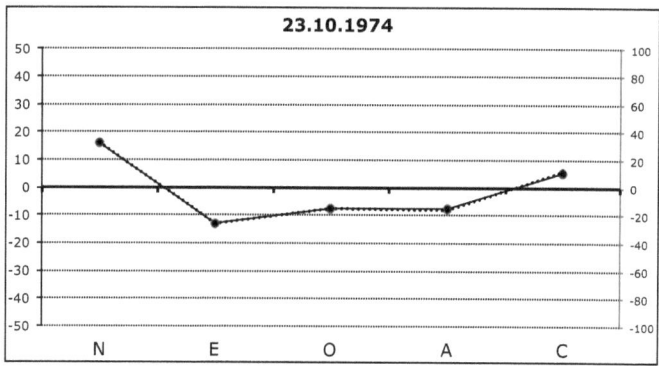

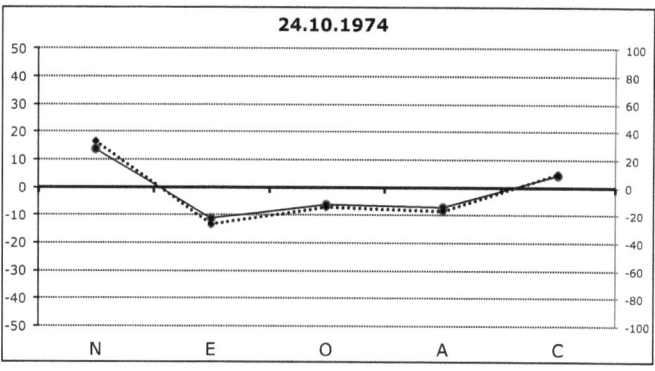

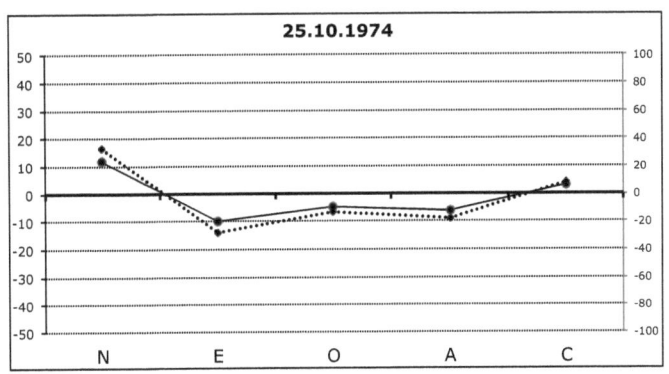

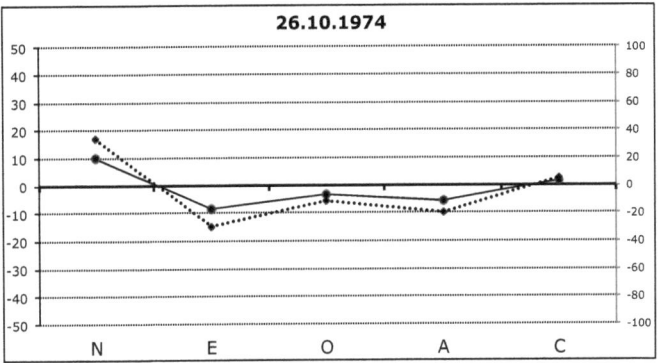

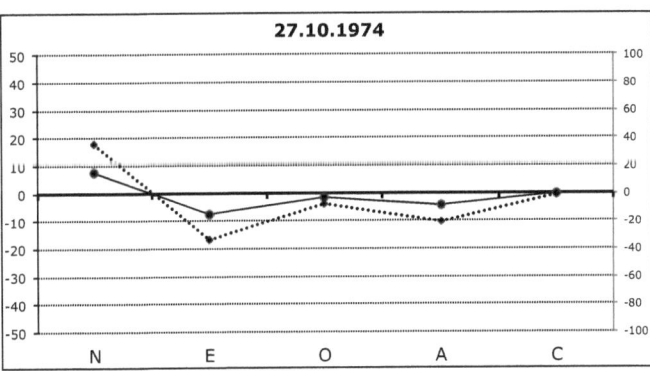

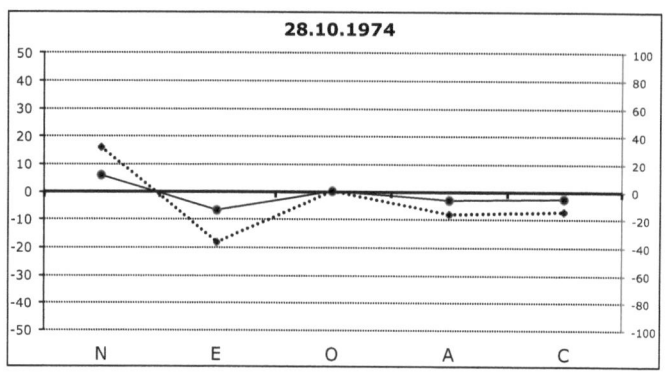

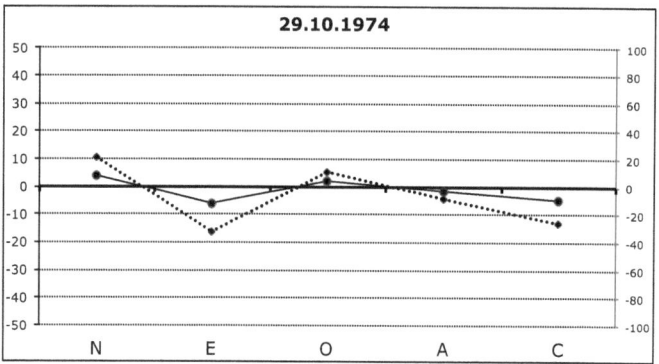

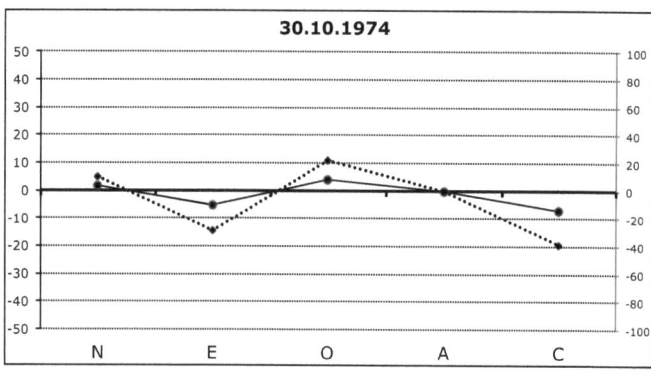

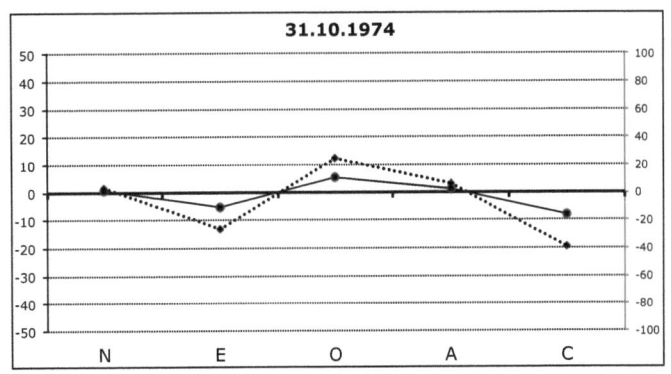

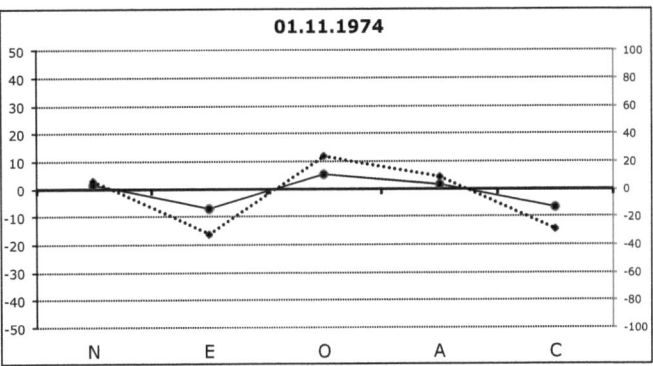

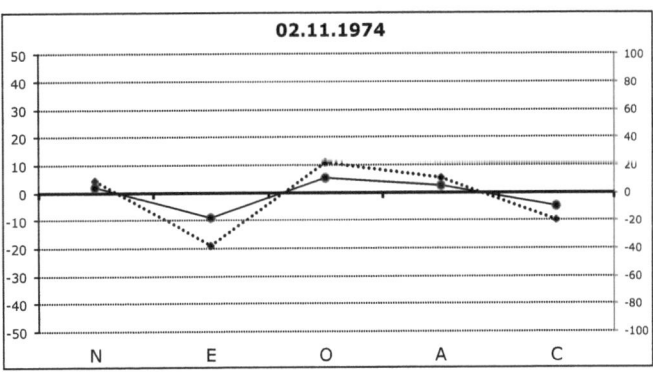

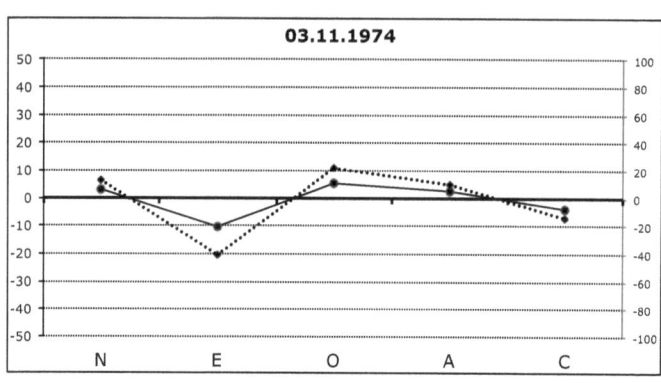

03.11.1974

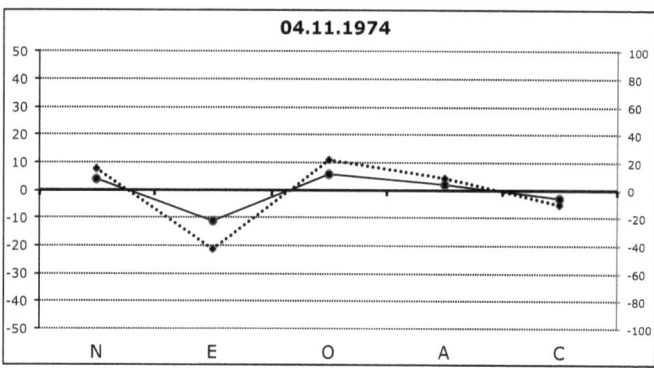

04.11.1974

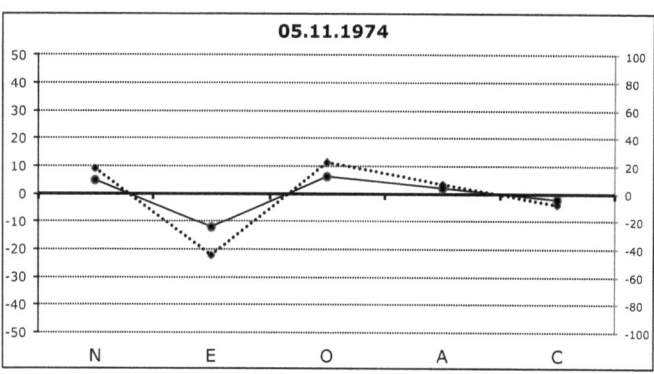

05.11.1974

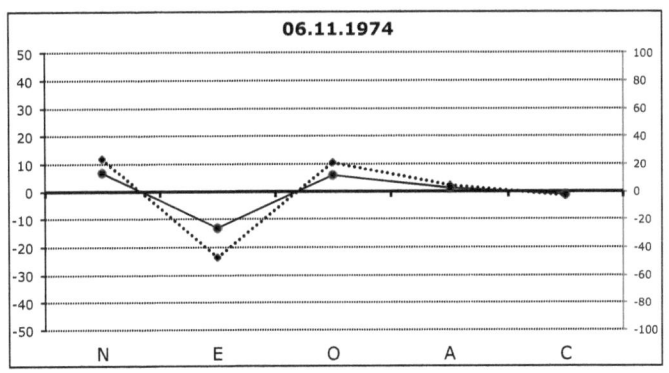

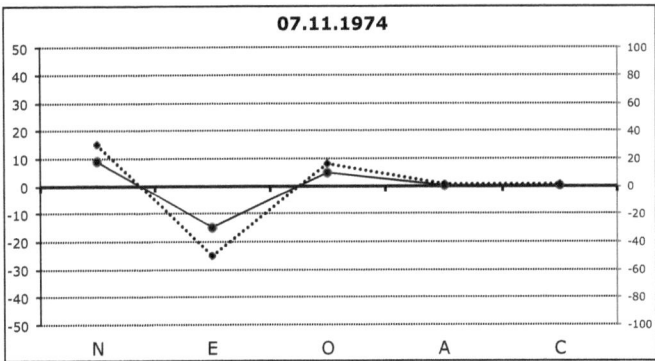

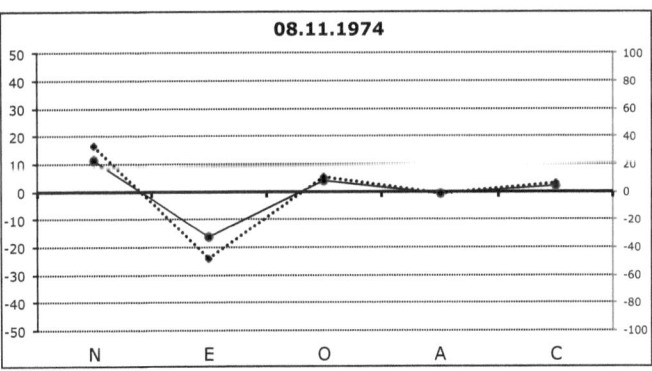

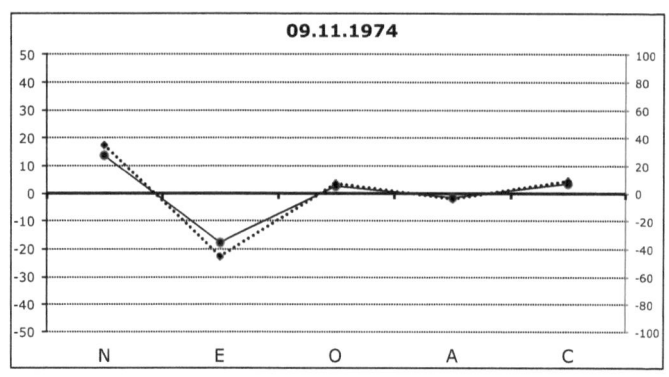

09.11.1974

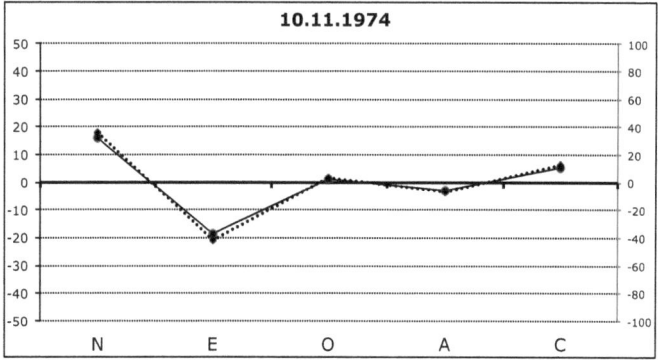

10.11.1974

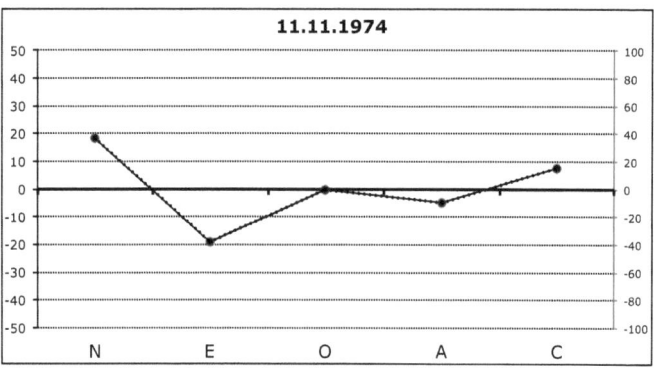

11.11.1974

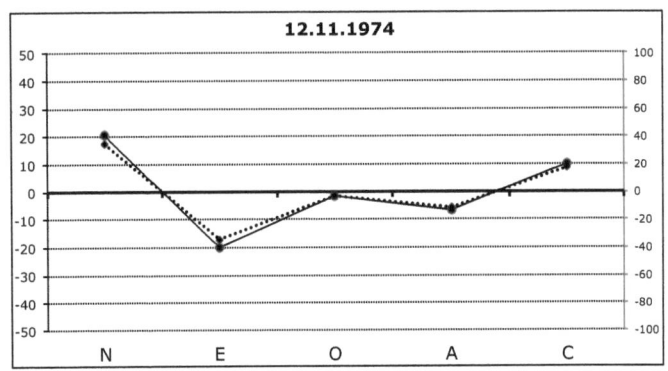

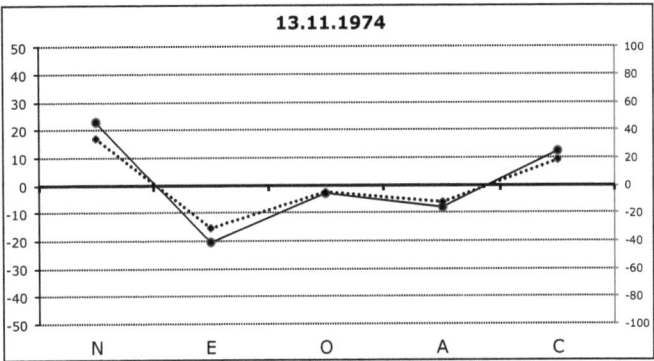

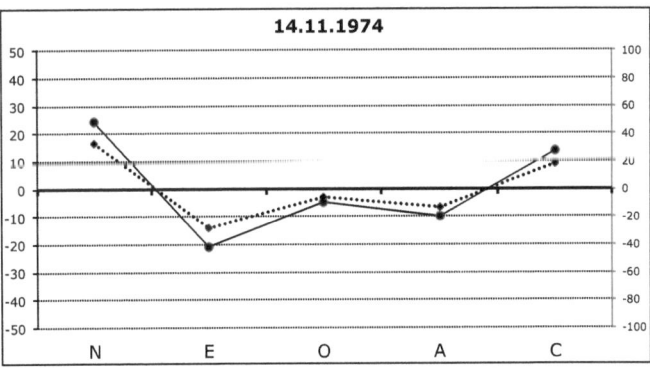

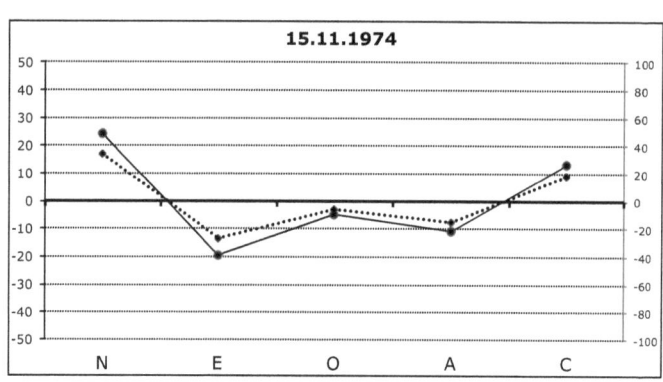

15.11.1974

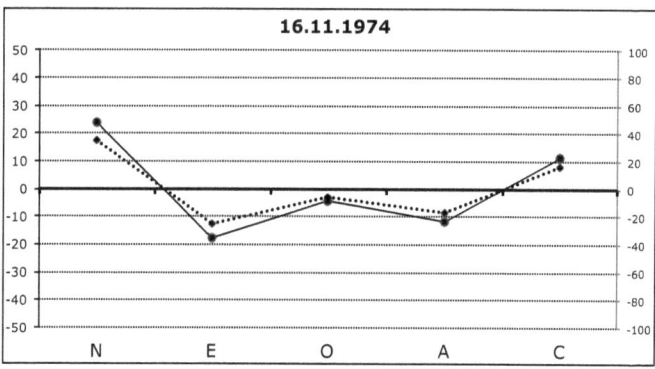

16.11.1974

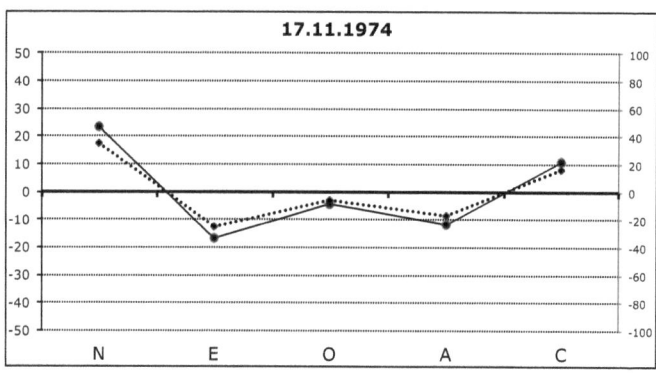

17.11.1974

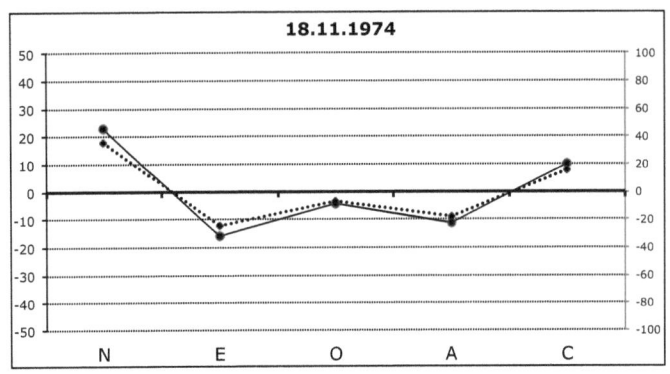

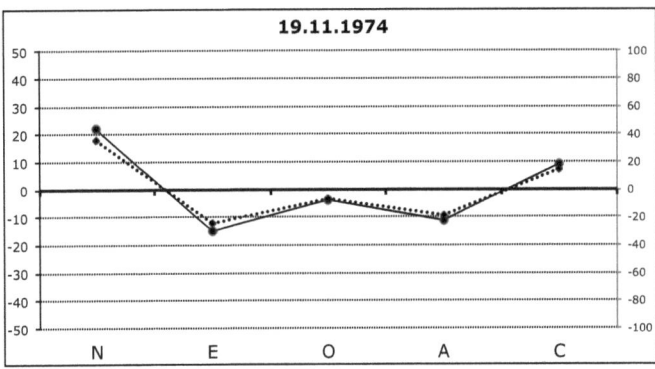

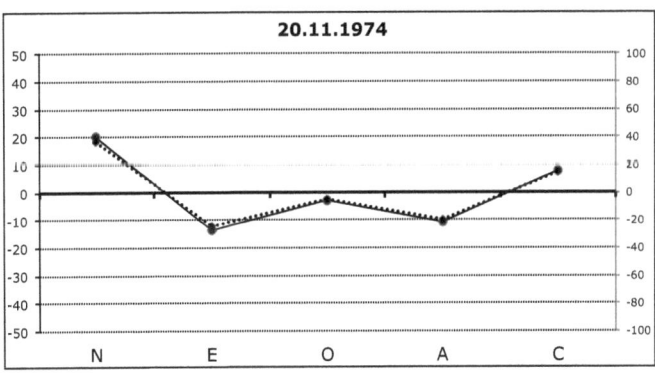

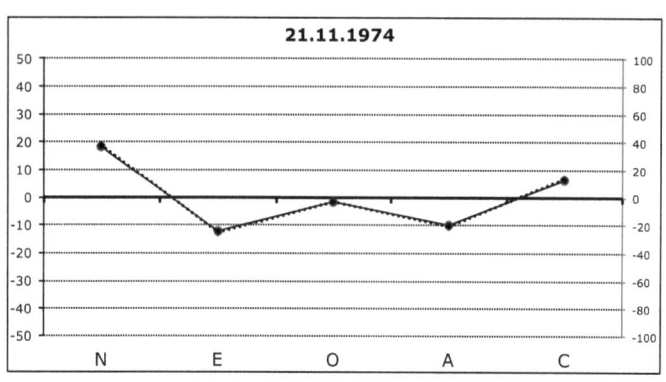

21.11.1974

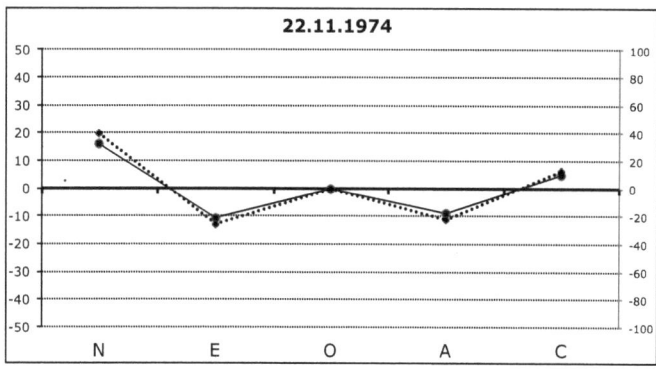

22.11.1974

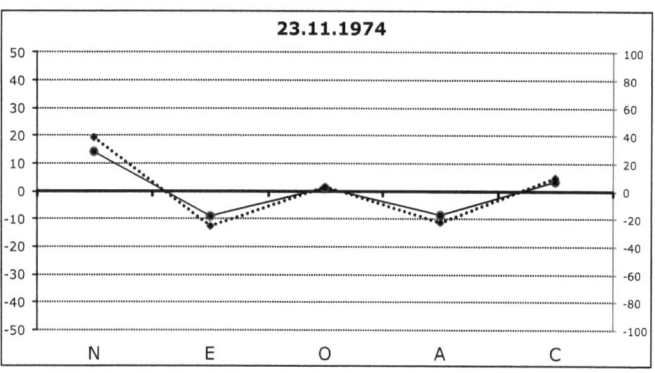

23.11.1974

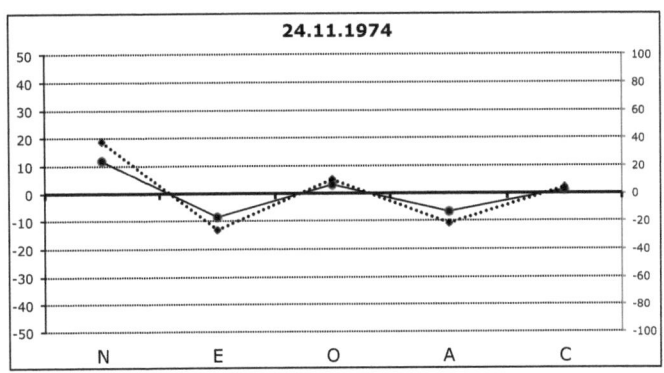

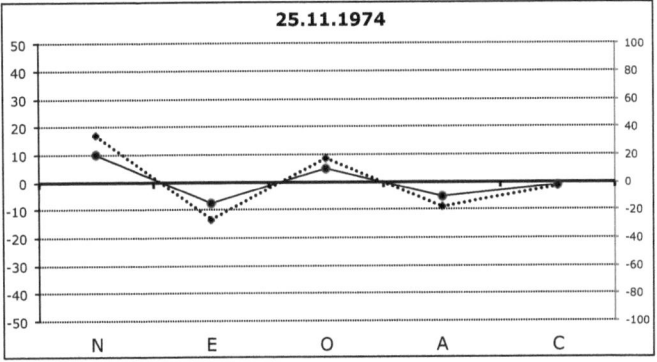

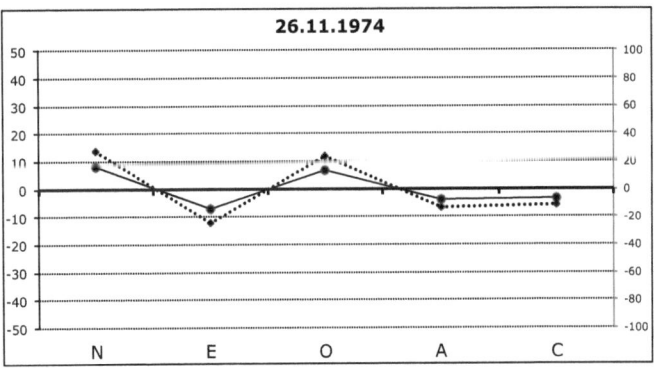

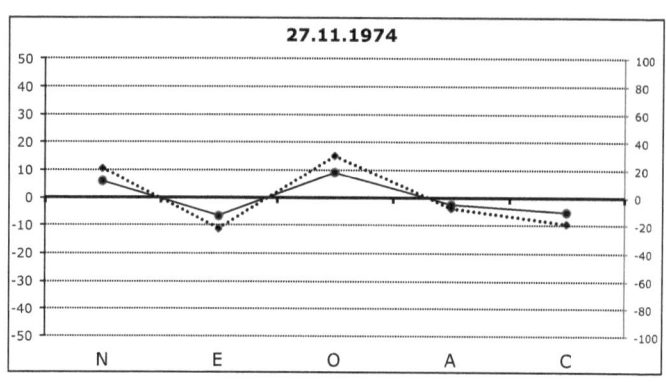

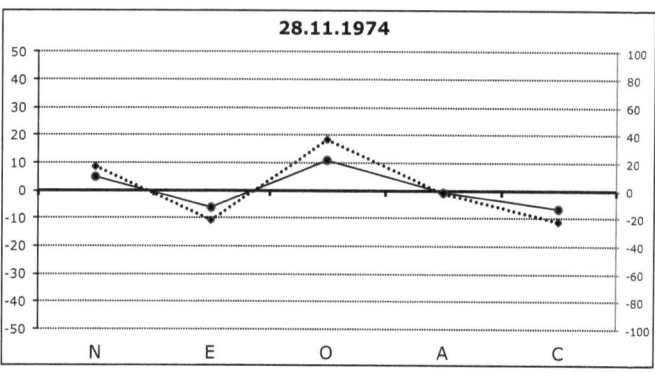

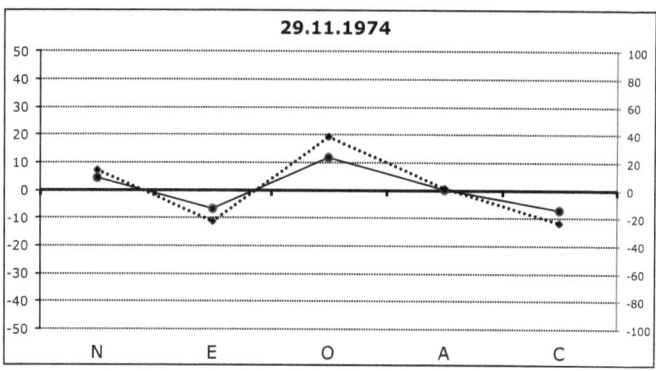

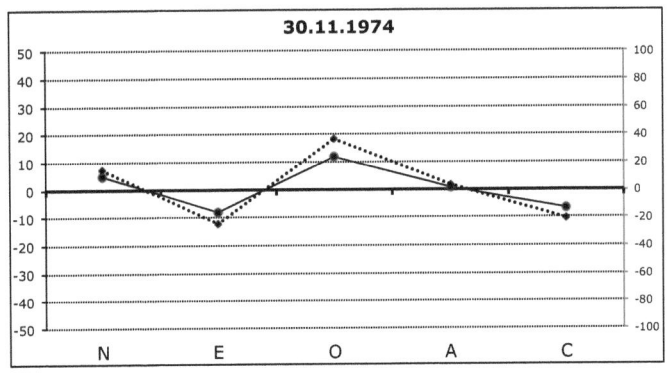

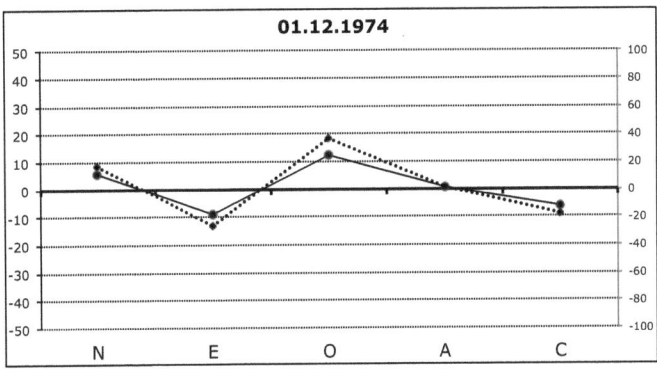

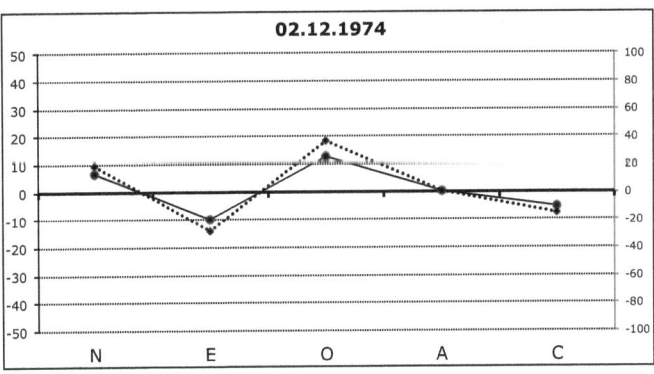

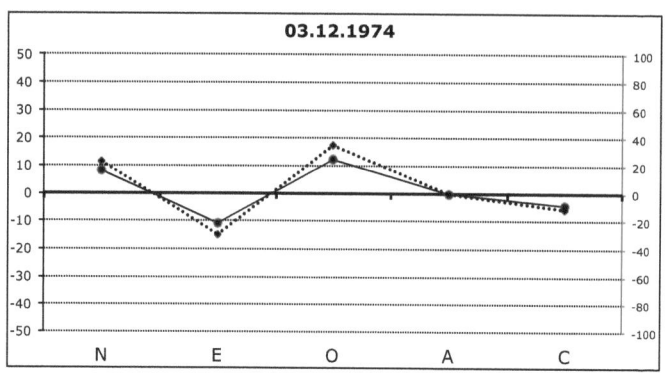

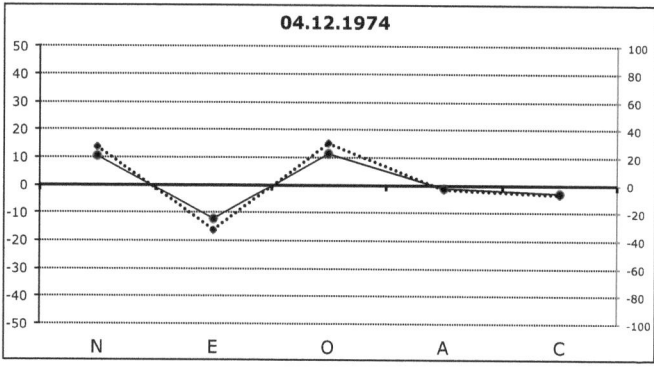

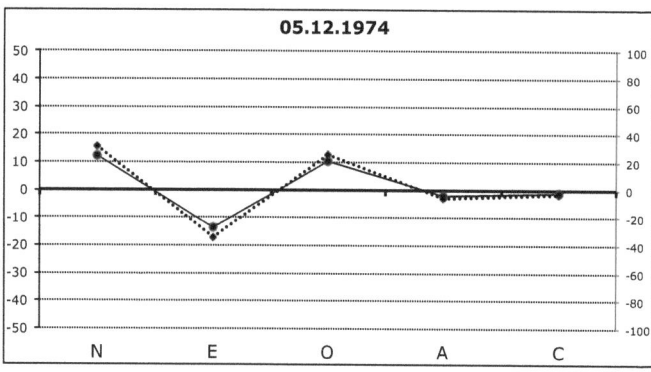

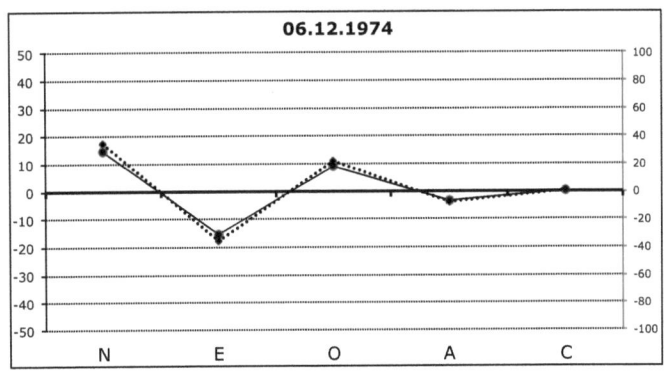

06.12.1974

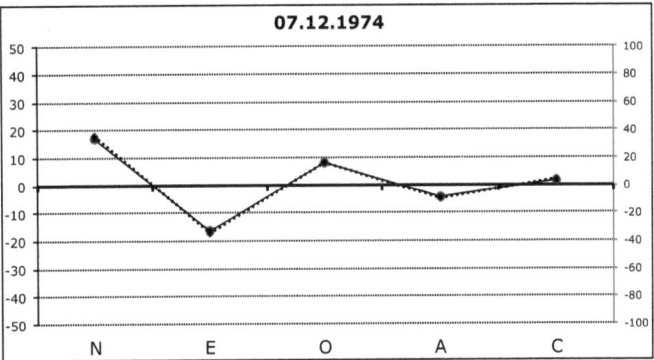

07.12.1974

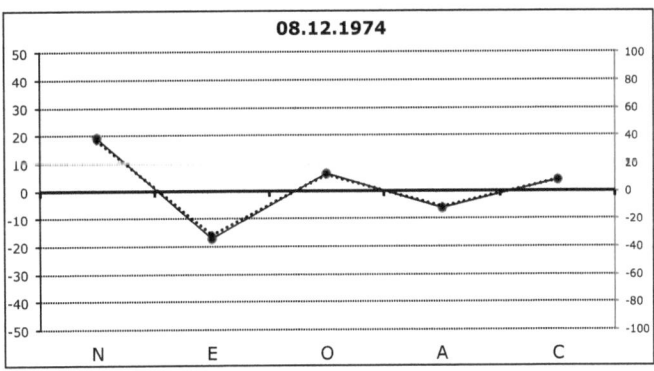

08.12.1974

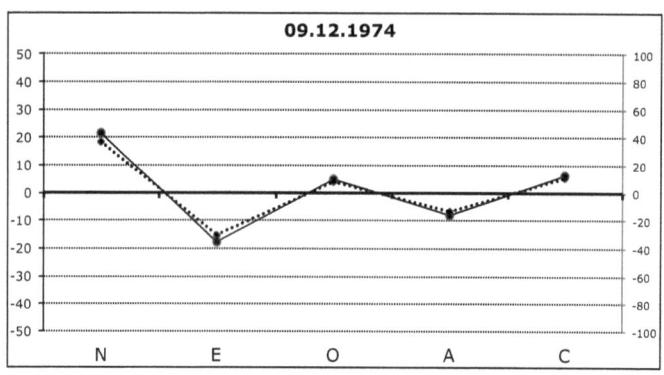

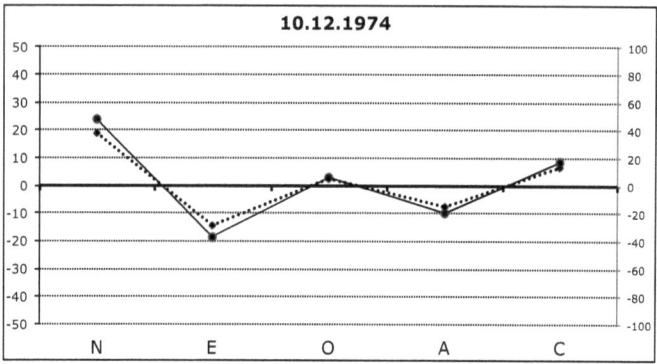

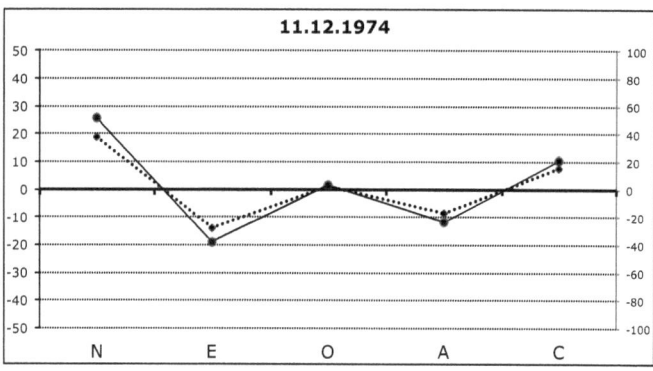

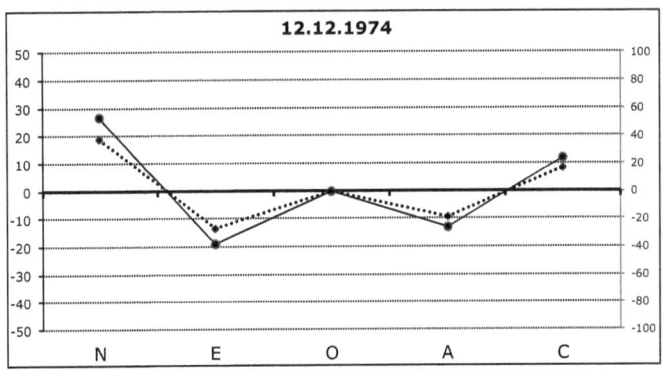

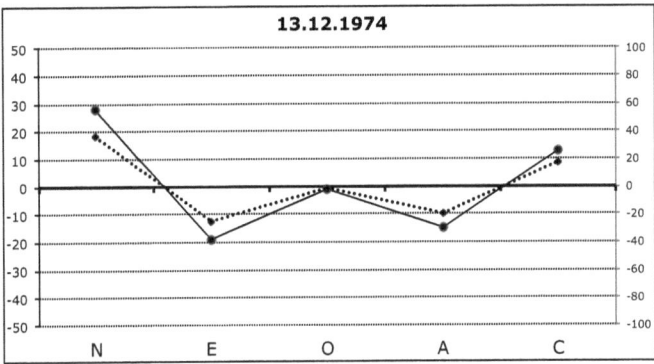

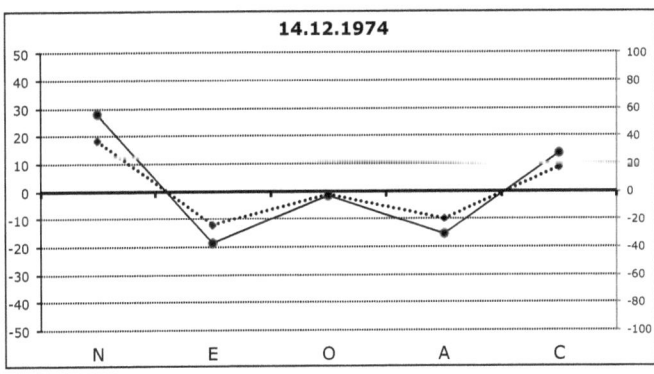

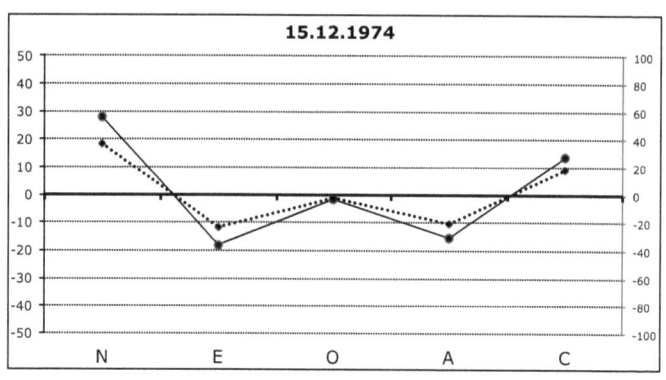

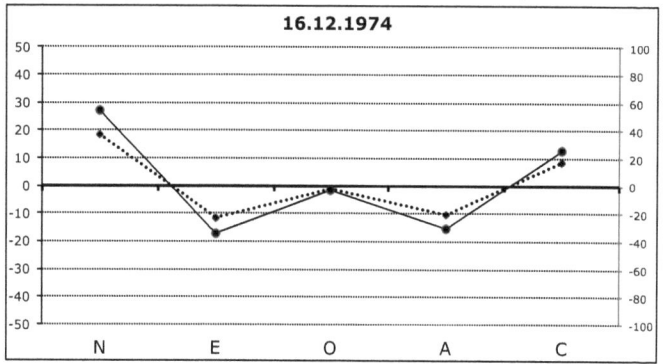

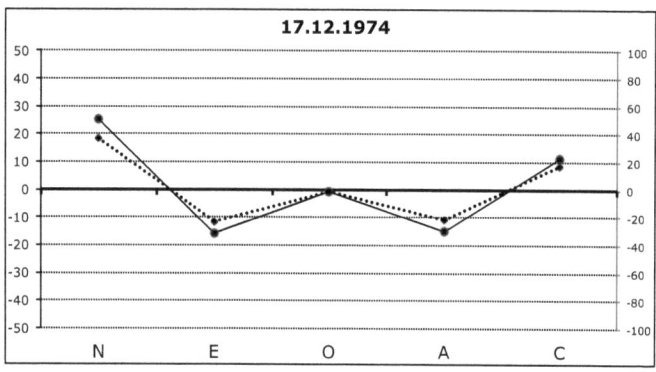

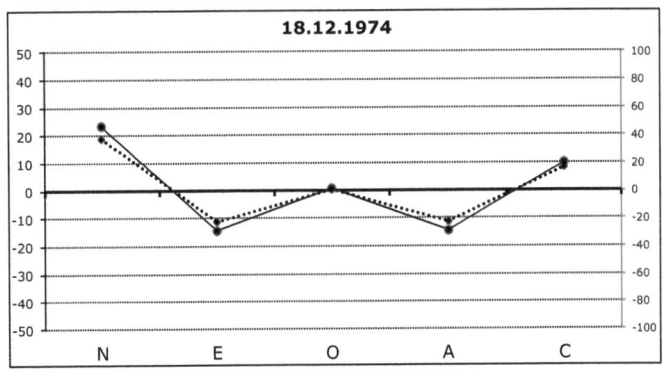

18.12.1974

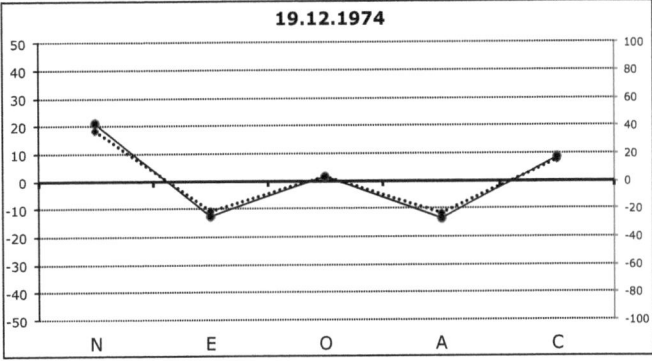

19.12.1974

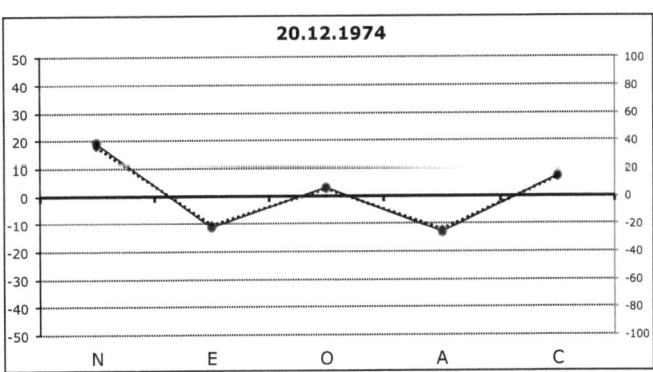

20.12.1974

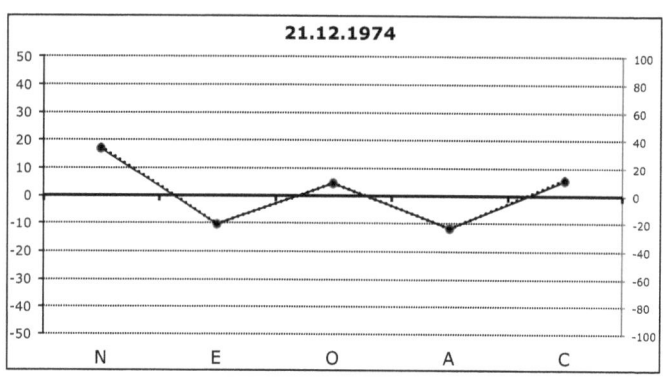

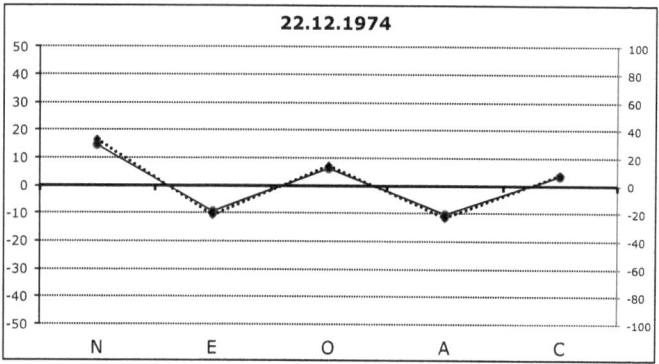

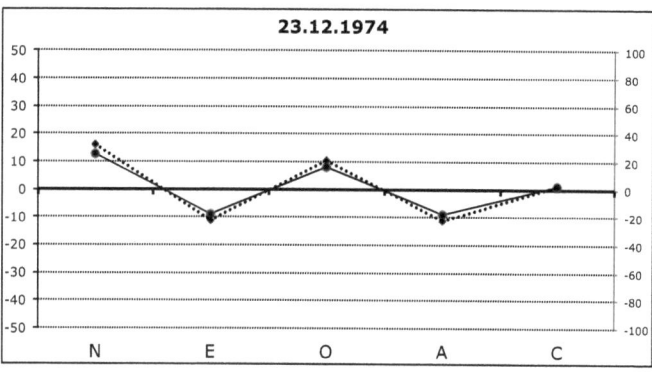

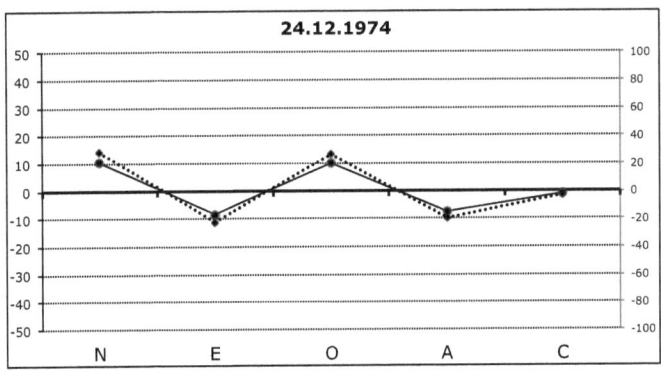

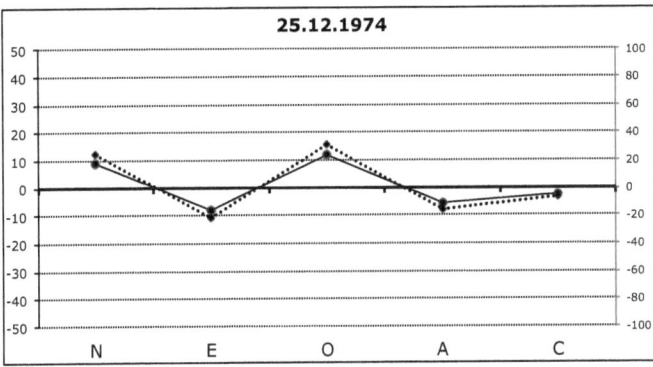

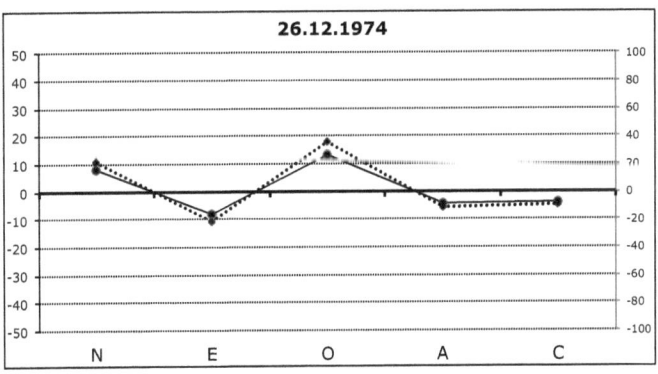

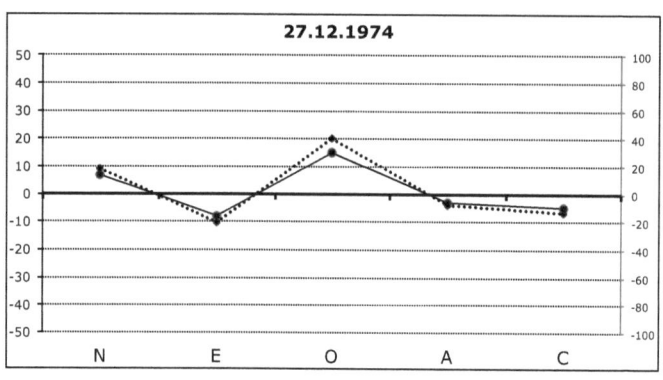

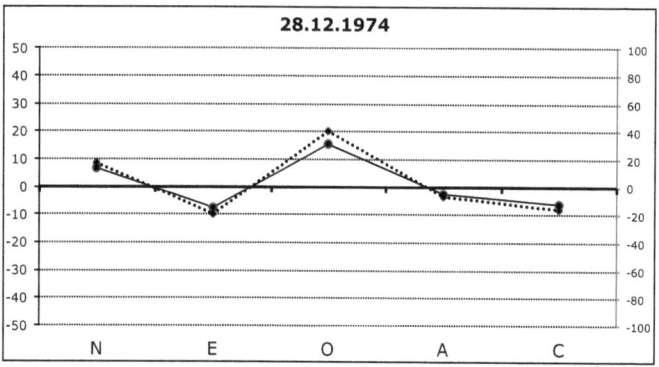

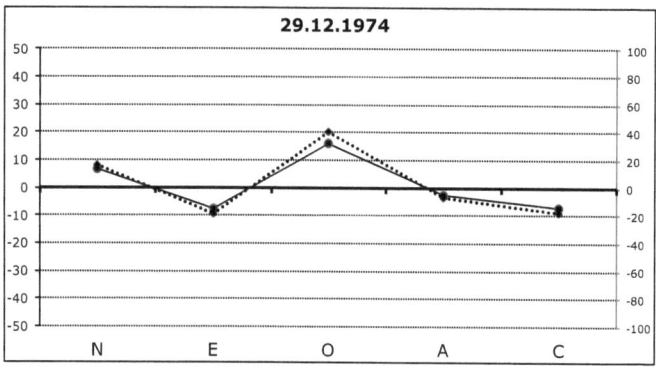

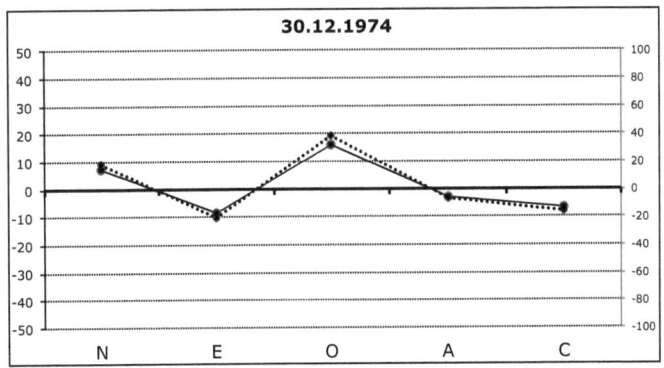

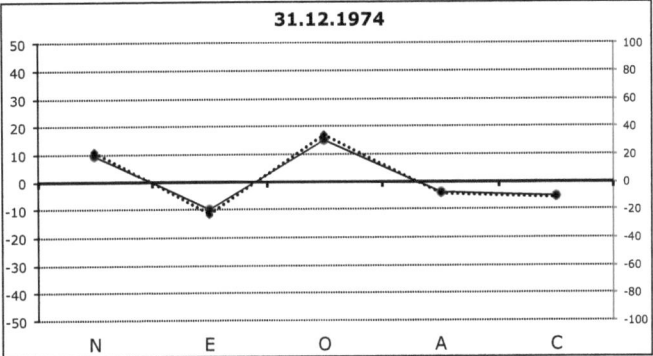

.